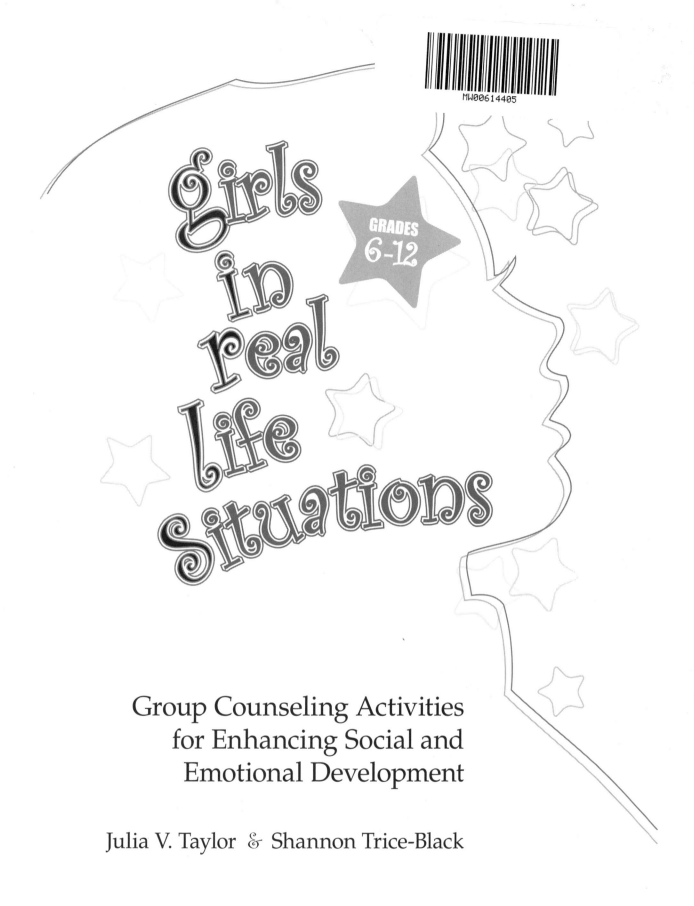

Girls in real life Situations

GRADES 6-12

Group Counseling Activities
for Enhancing Social and
Emotional Development

Julia V. Taylor & Shannon Trice-Black

Research Press | 2612 North Mattis Avenue | Champaign, Illinois 61822 | (800) 519-2707
www.researchpress.com

RESEARCH PRESS
PUBLISHERS

Copyright © 2007 by Julia V. Taylor and Shannon Trice-Black

9 8 7 6 5   13 14 15 16 17

All rights reserved. Printed in the United States of America.

In this volume, the following materials may be reproduced with proper credit to the source for noncommercial educational use by the original purchaser only, not to extend to reproduction by other parties:

"Ten Tips for G.I.R.L.S. Facilitators" (pp. 5–6)
and "G.I.R.L.S. Screening Interview (p. 7)

Lesson handouts

"Talk about It," "Think about It," and "Check It Out" pages

Appendixes A–E

Excerpts may be printed in connection with published reviews in periodicals without express permission. No other part of this book may be reproduced by any means without the written permission of the publisher.

Copies of this book may be ordered from Research Press at the address given on the title page.

Composition by Jeff Helgesen
Cover design by Linda Brown, Positive I.D. Graphic Design, Inc.
Printed by United Graphics, Inc.

ISBN: 978-0-87822-540-8
Library of Congress Control Number 2007928753

Contents

Appendixes

About the Authors

Acknowledgments

❀ Thank you to my wonderful family for shaping me into the person I am today.

❀ Thank you to Shannon Black, an amazing writer, role model, and friend.

❀ Thank you to Dr. Tamara Davis for everything. Words will never be able to express my gratitude.

❀ Thank you to the North Carolina School Counselor Association Board for your constant support and encouragement.

❀ Thank you to Wilma Keith; you are a true angel and inspiration.

❀ Thank you to the following remarkable women who have left a significant impression in my life: Tiffany McQueen, Jill Cook, Janine McGann, Leslie Edsall, Colleen Yeager, Alma Scoby, and Laura Read.

❀ Thank you to the girls that I have had the immense joy of working with. You all keep me energized and remind me every day of how much I have to learn!

❀ And to the memory of Laura Fitzsimmons; I hope this book somehow provides girls with the strength, courage, and coping skills to prevent another senseless loss.

—J.V.T

❀ Thank you, Lord, for continuing to guide me and for your faithfulness to me.

❀ Thank you, Julia Taylor—what a wonderful, amazing experience it is to have you as a friend and colleague.

❀ Thank you to my family, Gary, Margaret, and Caroline, for your love, patience, and laughter.

❀ Thank you to my parents, to Jennifer, and to Grandma for your prayers and encouragement.

❀ Thank you, Dr. Kathleen May and Dr. Linda Underwood, for being strong, independent, inspirational women.

❀ Thank you to my faithful friends, Liza, Kim, Marcy, Cheryl, Heather, Melodie, Shannon, and Kathy.

❀ Thank you to all girls everywhere!

—S.T.B.

About G.I.R.L.S.

In our fast-paced society, girls are often forced to grow up too quickly. As they navigate their turbulent adolescent years, girls frequently feel alone in their struggles. Girls in Real-Life Situations (G.I.R.L.S) is a group counseling curriculum designed to give girls an opportunity to feel empowered, gain self-awareness, develop positive coping mechanisms, improve daily problem-solving skills, feel connected with other girls, and make healthy decisions as they grow through turbulent times. This book includes activities appropriate for girls of middle and high school age.

In G.I.R.L.S., group members share feelings, struggles, and similarities and serve as a sounding board for one another while discussing and participating in a variety of activities dealing with issues common to all young women. The lesson plans and activities in this book are especially valuable to girls in the following circumstances:

❀ Special populations of girls who are struggling through their adolescent and teen years

❀ Girls in need of self-confidence

❀ Groups of friends who have trouble communicating with one another

❀ An entire community of girls who are interested in bonding on more than a superficial level

G.I.R.L.S. is intended primarily for use by school counselors, psychologists, social workers, and teachers but is also valuable to youth group leaders, Girl Scout leaders, health and fitness club coordinators, camp counselors, and anyone else interested in enhancing the social and emotional development of girls.

GROUP THEMES

G.I.R.L.S. facilitators may choose from 12 themes important to their particular population. These themes include topics important to all adolescent girls. The content of each is carefully designed to provoke thought and insight and promote a feeling of camaraderie while sharing personal experiences. Most important, the girls will have FUN!

1. Who Am I?
2. Body Image
3. Choices
4. Communication
5. Emotions
6. Friendships
7. Relationships
8. Self-Esteem
9. Stress
10. Reaching Out
11. Tough Times
12. Who I Am!

Each theme includes the following components.

Connect!

A 5- to 10-minute icebreaker activity is designed to introduce the topic about to be discussed in a fun, relaxed forum.

Lesson Plans

Each theme includes four different lesson plans from which to choose. Facilitators should consider the needs and interests of participants and the complexity of the issue when choosing the lesson or lessons.

Each lesson includes a rationale that explains the significance of the topic as well as step-by-step instructions for conducting the group. G.I.R.L.S. facilitators should review the rationales before each group session and summarize and personalize them as a way of introducing the girls to each topic. Each lesson should take approximately 45 minutes to complete—many involve supplemental handouts.

Talk about It

A "Talk about It" page presents a number of discussion questions. These discussion questions are designed to provoke thought and self-exploration about each theme. The discussion questions present a great forum for a high school group session, or they can be used at any time during a lesson plan as a supplement. The G.I.R.L.S. facilitator can read these questions aloud, or photocopy and cut apart the questions for girls to draw from a hat or bowl, and then discuss.

If the discussion questions alone are used for a group session, the facilitator can provide the "Think about It" and "Check It Out" pages, next described, at the end of the discussion for further self-exploration.

Think about It

A reproducible handout titled "Think about It," intended to encourage further soul searching about each theme, is also included. At the end of each handout are optional journaling questions. (Having the girls keep a journal is not necessary, but it does give them a healthy outlet to explore normative and self-beliefs.)

Check It Out

A "Check It Out" page lists books that supplement the session theme, for facilitators' or students' further exploration.

TEACHING OPTIONS

The G.I.R.L.S. curriculum can be used with small groups or, if desired, larger groups. In educational settings, the G.I.R.L.S. meetings can be held during lunch, before school, during a TA/activity period, or as an alternative to study hall. Prior to joining the G.I.R.L.S. group, each participant should receive a G.I.R.L.S. parent consent form (Appendix A) and confidentiality pledge (Appendix B), to be returned to the facilitator at a convenient time.

Small-Group Format

A small-group presentation of the G.I.R.L.S curriculum provides girls with a safe place to share and work through issues. In the small-group setting (4 to 12 participants—preferably an even number of girls), meetings approximately 45 minutes long should be conducted once a week over an 8- to 10-week period.

Each series of G.I.R.L.S. meetings should begin with the "Connect!" activity and an introduction to the chosen topic. The facilitator should then choose and conduct one or more lessons from the theme and end each theme with the "Talk about It," "Think about It," and "Check It Out" handouts. If facilitators plan to conduct multiple themes, it is suggested that the series begin with the theme "Who Am I?" and conclude with "Who I Am!"

Larger Groups

The G.I.R.L.S. materials can be adapted for use with larger groups at the facilitator's discretion. Such groups may include school clubs, Girl Scout troops, and girls attending a summer camp, among others. The discussion questions are a great way to share issues openly in a nonthreatening large-group format.

OTHER MATERIALS IN THIS BOOK

In addition to a parent consent form and confidentiality pledge, this book includes other helpful materials: a pretest/posttest (Appendix C), a certificate of achievement (Appendix D), and a group evaluation (Appendix E).

Pretest/Posttest

A brief pretest/posttest is included to help facilitators to determine the progress girls make from participating in G.I.R.L.S. Before conducting the first lesson, facilitators should administer the measure as a pretest, stressing the importance of honesty in the girls' responses. The measure can be administered again as a posttest during the final lesson. In addition to determining progress, comparisons between the pretest and posttest can help establish accountability.

Certificate of Achievement

The certificate of achievement gives group members an enthusiastic congratulation for their efforts and a reminder of their participation that they will be proud take home.

Group Evaluation

The group evaluation is intended to help the facilitator determine how the group went and to provide insight for any changes that might need to be made before selecting a new group of students. Girls may complete this evaluation at the same time they take the posttest or shortly thereafter.

Ten Tips for G.I.R.L.S. Facilitators

1. Begin each group by having everyone state the confidentiality pledge. Make sure the girls understand that what they share in the group will remain in the group unless you feel they are a danger to themselves or someone else and must refer them to a professional for help.

2. Always validate the girls' feelings. Validating their feelings will comfort them and encourage them to continue to participate in the group. You can validate their feelings both verbally and nonverbally.

3. During discussions, allow the girls to talk freely. Be sure to ask directive questions if there is a lull in the conversation. Do not attempt to challenge "wrong" answers; oftentimes the girls will do this on their own. If you need to intervene, try to ask probing questions that will motivate the girls to explore different sides of a topic. In addition, always give the girls the right to "pass" if they are not comfortable sharing at any particular point. It's important to keep in mind that group cohesion takes time to build.

4. Encourage discussion by asking open-ended questions or having one of the G.I.R.L.S. group members share an experience that is on topic or similar to the experience you're discussing.

5. Remain conscientious about not sharing personal information or lecturing the girls. Oftentimes, justification and validation of their concerns is all that they are seeking.

6. If a G.I.R.L.S. member is silent for weeks at a time, or emotionally shuts down, it is best to approach her privately. You may want to say, "I have noticed that you have not said much the past few weeks. Is there something going on?" or "Today I noticed that you shut down and refused to talk. Would you like to talk now about what the group was discussing or about what may be bothering you?"

7. Let the girls know that you are available to talk before or after the group session—or some other time, depending on your schedule—about issues brought up in the group.

8. Begin and end each session on time. Allow enough time at the end of the session for the girls to process and internalize what they have discussed.

From *Girls in Real-Life Situations: Group Counseling Activities for Enhancing Social and Emotional Development—Grades 6–12*
© 2007 by J. V. Taylor and S. Trice-Black. Champaign, IL: Research Press. (800–519–2707, www.researchpress.com)

9. Allow everyone the opportunity to share and be watchful of group dominators. If the behavior of a few girls becomes a problem for the group as a whole, speak to them individually or consider using a tool (such as a speaking stick, wand, etc.) so everyone has a chance to speak.

10. Have fun! Remember your days in middle school and high school and enjoy the opportunity you have to help girls bond together, use their voices, feel heard, and learn to trust one another.

G.I.R.L.S. Screening Interview

The following is a suggested screening procedure for G.I.R.L.S. facilitators to use when meeting with a potential G.I.R.L.S. member:

1. Introduce yourself.
2. Describe the rationale for and purpose of G.I.R.L.S.
3. Describe why the candidate was chosen for possible participation in G.I.R.L.S.
4. Discuss the frequency and duration of the G.I.R.L.S. meetings.
5. Discuss the goals of G.I.R.L.S.
6. Discuss the time commitment required for G.I.R.L.S.
7. Discuss group guidelines (timeliness, respect, honesty, empathy, and openness).
8. Discuss confidentiality and the consequences if confidentiality is broken.
9. Assure the candidates that you will keep their participation confidential but that, for the safety and welfare of everyone in the group, there are limits to what you can keep private. (You must tell if someone in the group says or does something that indicates she is at risk of harming others or herself.)
10. Ask the candidate the following questions:

    ❀ Do you think you are interested in G.I.R.L.S.?

    ❀ How do you feel G.I.R.L.S. will benefit you?

    ❀ What do you think you can offer other participants?

    ❀ Do you think you can follow the required guidelines?

    ❀ Are you willing to make up any assignments, tests, or quizzes if you have to miss them because of personal circumstances?

    ❀ Do you have any questions?

    If the potential member shows an interest in participating in G.I.R.L.S. and agrees to adhere to the guidelines and confidentiality requirements, give her a consent form so she can have a parent or guardian review, sign, and return it to you before the group sessions get under way.

From *Girls in Real-Life Situations: Group Counseling Activities for Enhancing Social and Emotional Development—Grades 6–12*
© 2007 by J. V. Taylor and S. Trice-Black. Champaign, IL: Research Press. (800–519–2707, www.researchpress.com)

Who Am I?

Who Am I?

Time

    10 minutes

Objective

    To build trust among group members

Materials

    Masking tape

Activity

    Before beginning, place two long lines of masking tape on either side of the room. Everyone stands side by side, on one side of the room. Tell the girls that they cannot speak during this activity. Read a statement from the list below and have the girls who have experienced what you read walk to the line, hold hands for a few seconds, and then return to the line. If space is limited, this activity may be altered to "Stand up if . . ."

Walk to the line . . .

- If you like the color red
- If you like pizza
- If you watch reality shows
- If you play a sport
- If you play an instrument
- If you have ever been in a car accident
- If you have ever cried yourself to sleep
- If your parents are divorced
- If you have ever gotten an F in school
- If you have ever thought you were fat
- If you have ever been made fun of because of the way you looked
- If you wished your hair was different

❀ If you have had a crush on a boy who didn't like you back

❀ If you have ever been in a fight with your best friend

❀ If you have ever been in a big fight with your parents and said something you regretted

❀ If you have ever been to Disney World

❀ If you have ever been terrified

❀ If you have ever judged someone based on their appearance

❀ If you have ever judged someone because of their race

❀ If you have ever wanted to be part of a group of more popular girls

❀ If you have ever lied to your mom or dad

❀ If you journal

❀ If you wished you were thinner

❀ If your parents have ever betrayed your trust

❀ If your friends have ever betrayed your trust

❀ If you have ever cheated on homework or on a test

❀ If you have ever lied to your friends

❀ If you have ever felt peer pressure

❀ If you have ever dressed in a particular way to impress your friends

❀ If you have ever cried because you felt out of control

❀ If you know someone who has cut themselves

❀ If you know an adult that drinks a lot or does drugs

❀ If you know of another student that drinks or does drugs

❀ If you sometimes don't really know who you are

Process Question
❀ Name one thing that surprised you about this connection activity.

Power Thinking

RATIONALE

Power thinking is positive self-talk that encourages and promotes a healthy thought process. It is valuable because girls tend to be quick to talk about what they believe to be their negative qualities. As a result, they have a difficult time seeing and verbalizing their individual self-worth and value. Designing power-thinking cards encourages each girl to articulate her valuable qualities and helps to promote in her a continual feeling of self-confidence.

MATERIALS

A set of Power Cards for each girl

Pencils or pens

Crayons or colored markers

PROCEDURE

1. Begin a discussion about the difference between positive and negative self-talk.

2. Ask each girl to talk about a time she accomplished something she is proud of. When all of the girls have had a turn, encourage them to reflect upon their individual qualities that helped them to accomplish what they discussed. Encourage the girls to share briefly what they came up with.

3. Talk about power thinking and explain the three different ways they can be used by the girls: *I am* (a statement of who they are), *I can* (a statement of what they can accomplish, and *I will* (a statement of self-belief.) Examples of each statement include the following:

    ❀ I am smart, I am a great soccer player, I am funny, and I am a great friend.

    ❀ I can get through rough times, I can help out my friends, I can control my actions, and I can believe in myself.

❀ I will like myself more, I will be more helpful to my parents, I will succeed in school, and I will eventually be a teacher.

4. Give each girl a Power Card from each of the three categories and encourage her to write a power-thinking statement in each square. If any of the girls is having trouble with the statements, encourage the other girls to help her. The girls can decorate their cards if time allows.

5. When they are all finished, invite the girls to share their power-thinking statements with the group.

6. Encourage the girls to place the cards in their lockers, on their mirrors, in their rooms, in their diaries, or in their scrapbooks or to carry them in their backpacks or purses. Also remind them to repeat their power-thinking statements often!

CLOSING QUESTIONS

❀ Why do girls often struggle with talking about their positive qualities?

❀ What are some ways you can combat your negative thinking with positive thinking?

❀ How will you use what you have learned today in the future?

Power Cards

Copy and cut out the following cards. Give one card from each category to each girl.

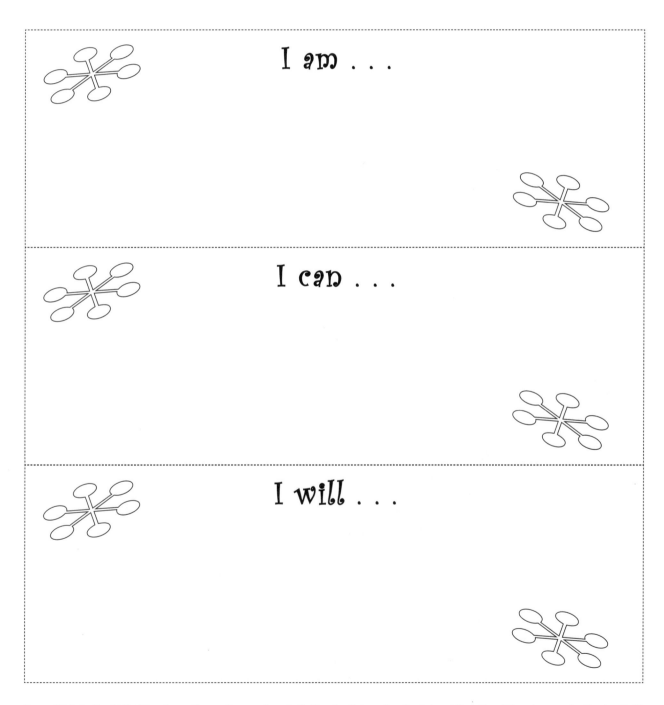

I am . . .

I can . . .

I will . . .

From *Girls in Real-Life Situations: Group Counseling Activities for Enhancing Social and Emotional Development—Grades 6–12*
© 2007 by J. V. Taylor and S. Trice-Black. Champaign, IL: Research Press. (800–519–2707, www.researchpress.com)

Masks

RATIONALE

Girls are notorious for comparing themselves to others, and so they wear different masks or put on different faces, depending on the particular norms of the social situation they are in. Masks provide a comforting way for them to hide their true selves and fit in, and they serve as a protective barrier to avoid getting hurt. Girls often go through tumultuous times and experience a roller coaster of emotions, leaving them more vulnerable to loss of identity. This activity allows the girls to analyze, demonstrate, and explore the different ways they act around the important people in their lives.

MATERIALS

Paper plates (at least three for each girl)

Magazines or newspapers

Pencils or pens

Colored markers

Optional: Craft sticks, glue or tape

PROCEDURE

1. Prior to discussion, hand each girl a copy of the pretest and allow her enough time to complete it. Stress the importance of honesty! Collect all pretests and save them to compare to posttests, which will be completed during the last session.

2. Begin with a discussion about why girls wear masks.

3. Ask the girls to think about the masks they wear and how they change daily. Provoke thought about how they act at home, school, and social events and around friends, boys, strangers, teachers, and others.

4. Hand out the materials and have each girl decorate three masks, with each mask representing how she presents herself most often.

5. When all the girls have finished, ask them to discuss their masks and how they change from day to day and situation to situation. If you use craft sticks, the girls can attach them to their masks so they can hold the masks up to their faces when describing the different situations in which they wear them.

CLOSING QUESTIONS

❀ Which mask do you feel most comfortable in?

❀ Which mask would you like to get rid of?

❀ How will you use what you have learned today in the future?

Self-Portraits

RATIONALE

Self-portraits offer girls a creative outlet to express how they view themselves in a nonthreatening format. In addition, self-portraits will provide the G.I.R.L.S. facilitator with a deeper understanding of everyone's background. This activity is duplicated during the last group session so the two self-portraits can be compared.

MATERIALS

A copy of the Self-Portrait of _____ handout for each girl

Pencils or pens

Crayons or colored markers

Optional: glue, sand, and glitter

PROCEDURE

1. Ask the girls to close their eyes and picture themselves. Encourage each girl to consider how she feels about her body, home life, school, friends, and social activities. Give everyone a few minutes to grasp an image.

2. Give each girl the Self-Portrait handout and distribute the art supplies.

3. Tell the girls that when they have come up with an image, they should open their eyes and, to the best of their ability, draw that image on paper.

4. Allow the girls to talk freely with one another, but not about their portraits. When everyone has completed the assignment, ask each girl to describe her portrait to the group.

CLOSING QUESTIONS

❧ How is your portrait different from the image you project to others?

❀ What is a step you are willing to take to improve your vision of yourself?

❀ How will you use what you have learned today in the future?

Self-Portrait of _____

From *Girls in Real-Life Situations: Group Counseling Activities for Enhancing Social and Emotional Development—Grades 6–12*
© 2007 by J. V. Taylor and S. Trice-Black. Champaign, IL: Research Press. (800–519–2707, www.researchpress.com)

Role Models

RATIONALE

Girls often identify with other females as role models and copy behaviors, dress, interests, and hobbies. They often have difficulty finding and relating to appropriate role models who can help them face the future with a positive, healthy outlook. Furthermore, it can be difficult for them to find role models from diverse backgrounds to whom they can relate. Girls need healthy role models who place importance on friendship, responsibility, decision making, sports, academics, and community service. Positive role models can help girls deal with the many complex issues and decisions that are an intrinsic part of growing up. This activity encourages girls to explore appropriate role models, with whom they can identify.

MATERIALS

A copy of the Women Who ROCK! handout for each girl

Pencils or pens

PROCEDURE

1. Begin with a discussion of the many positive female role models in our society. Encourage the girls to discuss characteristics of appropriate role models and explain that positive role models do not need to be famous or extremely successful or fit a particular stereotype. Role models need to be strong females who are responsible, respectful, motivated, and honest.

2. Instruct the girls to think about a female who has been an encouraging role model to them.

3. Give each girl a copy of the Women Who ROCK! handout.

4. Instruct the girls to write the qualities of their role models in the squares. Encourage creativity!

5. When the girls have finished, have them share the characteristics of their role models with one another.

CLOSING QUESTIONS

❀ What are some characteristics of great role models?

❀ Do you think it is hard for girls to find appropriate, realistic role models?

❀ What are some things you have learned from your role model and applied to your own life?

❀ Is there anything that you would like to do differently so that you can be more like your role model? If so, please explain.

Women Who ROCK!

From *Girls in Real-Life Situations: Group Counseling Activities for Enhancing Social and Emotional Development—Grades 6–12*
© 2007 by J. V. Taylor and S. Trice-Black. Champaign, IL: Research Press. (800–519–2707, www.researchpress.com)

Who Am I?

1. Who are you? What defines who you are?
2. What is the best thing about being a girl?
3. How is being a girl different from being a boy?
4. Talk about a time when you wished you were not a girl.
5. What group of people do you like to hang out with?
6. What has been the most difficult part about getting older?
7. When do you pretend to be somebody else?
8. What are some qualities you judge other people on?
9. What are some of your short-term goals?
10. What do you hope to obtain from the G.I.R.L.S. group?
11. What are some things about you that are super-special?
12. Do you face challenges with a positive or negative attitude?
13. Talk about a time you wished you were someone different.
14. Who are your female role models? What makes you look up to and admire these women?
15. How do you want other people to see you?
16. When do you feel "fake"?
17. How does your personality change as you associate with different groups of people? Why do you think it changes?
18. Is it difficult to point out your good qualities to other people?
19. Is it easy to point out your flaws to other people?
20. How or where do you see yourself in 10 years? How will you get there?

From *Girls in Real-Life Situations: Group Counseling Activities for Enhancing Social and Emotional Development—Grades 6–12*
© 2007 by J. V. Taylor and S. Trice-Black. Champaign, IL: Research Press. (800–519–2707, www.researchpress.com)

Think about It

Who Am I?

What are three words that describe you?

1. _____

2. _____

3. _____

What are three words your friends would use to describe you?

1. _____

2. _____

3. _____

What are three words your family would use to describe you?

1. _____

2. _____

3. _____

In what ways are these words related?

_____

_____

_____

From *Girls in Real-Life Situations: Group Counseling Activities for Enhancing Social and Emotional Development—Grades 6–12*
© 2007 by J. V. Taylor and S. Trice-Black. Champaign, IL: Research Press. (800–519–2707, www.researchpress.com)

Who Am I? (continued)

In what ways are these words different?

_____

_____

_____

Directions: Using what you have learned in the group, write a short personal vision statement. A vision statement is a broad, inspirational message about what you are trying to achieve. Your vision statement should encompass your personal values and beliefs. For example, "I will always be true to family, friends, and myself" or "I will try to give my all every day." Your vision statement does not have to be long—just accurate and a true reflection of who you are.

_____

_____

_____

_____

_____

_____

Optional Journaling Questions

❀ What are your values?
❀ What are your beliefs?
❀ Who helped shape your values and beliefs?

Check It Out

Who Am I?

Here are some great books for teens. Check them out!

* *The 7 Habits of Highly Effective Teens,* by Sean Covey (New York: Fireside, 1998).

* *Daily Reflections of Highly Effective Teens,* by Sean Covey (New York: Fireside, 1999).

* *The Seven Best Things Smart Teens Do,* by John C. Friel and Linda D. Friel (Deerfield Beach, FL: Health Communications 2000).

* *Posers, Fakers, and Wannabes: Unmasking the Real You,* by Brennan Manning and Jim Hancock (Colorado Springs, CO: Navpress, 2003).

* *Deal with It! A Whole New Approach to Your Body, Brain, and Life as a gURL,* by Esther Drill, Heather McDonald, and Rebecca Odes (New York: Simon and Schuster, 1999).

From *Girls in Real-Life Situations: Group Counseling Activities for Enhancing Social and Emotional Development—Grades 6–12*
© 2007 by J. V. Taylor and S. Trice-Black. Champaign, IL: Research Press. (800–519–2707, www.researchpress.com)

Body Image

Connect!

Body Image

Time

10 minutes

Objective

For each girl to say something positive about her body

Materials

Container or cup

Slips of paper and pencil

Preparation

Write a different letter of the alphabet on separate slips of paper. Fold the slips and place them in the container or cup.

Activity

Everyone stands or sits in a circle. As the container or cup is passed around the circle, each girl picks out a slip of paper. Each girl then describes something positive about her body that begins with the letter written on the paper. For example, for the letter *A*, a girl could say, "I like my arm," or she could use a descriptive adjective such as *adorable.*

Process Questions

❀ Did you find this exercise difficult? Explain why or why not.

❀ Why do you think it is important for girls to say positive things about themselves?

Beating the Body-Image Blues

RATIONALE

Girls are notorious for making negative remarks and thinking negatively about their bodies. They might say, for example, "I feel fat," "My legs are so huge," "I am so ugly," "I hate my hair," "My nose is so big," and so on. Girls emotionally reason with themselves, believing that how they feel is reality. For example, "If I feel ugly, I AM ugly." In this activity, each girl will learn how to identify underlying feelings when making a negative remark about her body and will challenge the negative thought with an appropriate positive thought.

MATERIALS

A copy of Beating Bad Body Thoughts handout for each girl
Pencils or pens

PROCEDURE

1. Begin by asking the girls how many of them have made the following statements:

   "I am SO ugly!"

   "I feel FAT!"

   "My legs are HUGE!"

   "My hair looks SO bad!"

   "I have BAD skin!"

   "I ate TOO much!"

   You may add anything else that may pertain to your particular group.

2. Give each girl a copy of the Beating Bad Body Thoughts handout.

3. In a roundtable format, challenge the girls to think about the last time they had a negative body thought and to describe the setting, their thought process, and what led them to that feeling.

4. For every "bad body thought" they have, they must come up with a "good body thought" to help them combat the negative thought.

CLOSING QUESTIONS

❀ What are you really feeling when you criticize your body?

❀ What are you willing to do to praise your body on a regular basis?

❀ How will you use what you have learned today in the future?

Beating Bad Body Thoughts

Directions: Think about all the times you say or think something bad about your body. For each negative statement, you must come up with something positive to say to help you squash those bad body thoughts!

Bad Body Thought	Good Body Thought

From *Girls in Real-Life Situations: Group Counseling Activities for Enhancing Social and Emotional Development—Grades 6–12* © 2007 by J. V. Taylor and S. Trice-Black. Champaign, IL: Research Press. (800–519–2707, www.researchpress.com)

Mixed Media Messages

RATIONALE

Girls are exposed to thousands of media images that can negatively influence how they feel about themselves. Women portrayed in the media generally have unattainable images that young girls idolize. Advertisements are designed to make young girls believe that their lives will be better if they own a certain product or look like the person selling a particular product. This activity is designed to help girls realize that the media industry is a business and that images are designed, corrected, and perfected to market merchandise.

MATERIALS

Magazines including plenty of advertisements (make sure they are girl-friendly and include popular media)

Scissors and glue

Colored markers

Posterboard

PROCEDURE

1. Have all art materials accessible to the girls upon their arrival.
2. Instruct the girls to go through the magazines and cut out the advertising images they like.
3. When they are finished, have them work together to create a collage on the posterboard. Encourage creativity through use of words, language, and images that are inviting and enticing to the girls.
4. When the collage is finished, have each girl describe to the group what she likes about it and what was attractive about her choices.
5. Ask the girls some of the following questions to help explore the critical and mixed messages that the media project:
   - ❀ What are some of the facial expressions on the collage? Do you think the media want you to believe that you will feel a certain way if you own the product?

- Have you ever bought something advertised in the media only to be disappointed?

- How do you feel about yourself after you read a magazine or book with really pretty girls in it?

- How many mixed messages can you think of that the media send us daily? For example, they constantly present us with fast-food ads and commercials, but at the same time tell us we should not eat fast food.

- Do magazine and television advertisements tell the truth? Why or why not?

- What types of things do media companies do to make people look better?

- If average people were in magazines and television shows, do you think the products they are selling would be as popular as they are now?

Steer the discussion toward the "business" side of the media, meaning that the media exist to make a profit.

CLOSING QUESTIONS

- Are the images the media portray reality?

- Do you think this activity may change the way you feel about the media?

- How will you use what you have learned today in the future?

She's All That

RATIONALE

Girls are exposed to thousands of teen celebrities, fashion icons, beauty products, and diet commercials that enforce the notion that their body shape, size, and fashion sense determine success. In addition, girls often judge others solely on their looks and the size of their bodies. In this lesson, the girls will discuss healthy women in their lives and the characteristics, besides beauty, that make them attractive.

MATERIALS

Paper and pencils or pens

Easel pad or posterboard

A copy of the My Standards of Success handout for each girl

PROCEDURE

1. Have the paper and pencils or pens ready to hand out before the girls arrive.
2. Before beginning the session, ask the girls to write down the names of five women they personally know who are either average size (or larger) and whom they look up to or admire.
3. When they are finished, have them turn their papers over.
4. Ask the girls to describe the "perfect girl," a girl that is "all that." Write their responses on the easel pad or posterboard.
5. Ask for a volunteer (or the entire group) to demonstrate the actions of the "perfect girl." How does she act, how does she laugh, how does she sit, and so forth.
6. When they are done, have each girl read aloud the names of the women they wrote down and why they admire them.
7. Ask the girls if the characteristics that they recalled were similar to the characteristics of the girls they believe are "perfect" or think they are "all that."

8. When the girls have discussed this point, give each one a copy of the My Standards of Success handout.

9. Encourage the girls to use interpersonal qualities, as opposed to external features, in their list, as in the qualities of the women they listed.

CLOSING QUESTIONS

❀ What have you learned about yourself and the judgments you make about other girls?

❀ Has this activity changed the way you plan to think about girls and women who don't have perfect bodies?

❀ How will you use what you have learned today in the future?

My Standards of Success

Directions: Think about the qualities of everyday women you admire. List their amazing qualities below and the qualities that define a truly successful woman.

_____

_____

_____

_____

_____

_____

_____

_____

_____

_____

_____

_____

_____

_____

From *Girls in Real-Life Situations: Group Counseling Activities for Enhancing Social and Emotional Development—Grades 6–12*
© 2007 by J. V. Taylor and S. Trice-Black. Champaign, IL: Research Press. (800–519–2707, www.researchpress.com)

Fill Her Up!

RATIONALE

Girls are very quick to point out what they do not like about their bodies. This activity teaches the girls to literally fill their bodies with positive thoughts.

MATERIALS

    A body-length sheet of paper for each girl

    Magazines and newspapers

    Scissors, glue

    Colored markers, paint, colored paper

    Optional: Glitter, feathers

PROCEDURE

1. Begin by asking the girls what they like about their bodies—ask them to refrain from saying anything negative.
2. After the discussion, either pair up the girls or ask them to get a partner.
3. Give each girl a long sheet of paper, have her lie down on it, and instruct her partner to trace around her body.
4. When they have completed tracing one another, instruct the girls to use the magazines, newspapers, and art supplies to fill their bodies with positive images, thoughts, colors, and phrases.
5. Encourage them to discuss the meaning of their images they put inside their bodies with their partner while they work.
6. Upon completion, have the girls present their partners project to the group.

CLOSING QUESTIONS

❀ Was it difficult to fill your entire body with positive things?

❀ What did this activity teach you about your body?

❀ How will you use what you have learned today in the future?

Talk about It

Body Image

1. What is your definition of *body image?* What are your thoughts and feelings about your body?

2. How did you form your thoughts (positive or negative) about your body?

3. Has anyone ever made a negative remark about your body? How did you respond? What were your afterthoughts or reactions?

4. When you are meeting someone for the first time, what is the first thing you judge?

5. The diet industry is a multibillion-dollar industry with an almost 100 percent failure rate. What are your thoughts about that? Would you buy a car that you thought would not start 98 percent of the time? Would you want a doctor to perform surgery on you who had been unsuccessful on 9 out of 10 patients?

6. Why do you think that girls have a hard time accepting their bodies?

7. What do you think about when you see a model with perfect skin selling an acne product or face wash that promises to make your skin look flawless?

8. Have you ever missed school, a party, or a sporting event because you didn't like how you looked?

9. Have you ever heard a song and thought of it one way and then seen the song portrayed in a music video in another fashion? How did you feel about the song afterward? What messages was the video trying to send?

10. Are you affected by other people's opinions about your body? How do you know what their opinions are?

11. Would you change any part of your body? If so, what would be different if that part was different?

12. What is the reality of the illegal things that happen on television and in the movies? For example, what could the possible consequences be for driving 100 miles per hour down a one-way street with a gun, on your cell phone, while drinking alcohol?

13. Do you think the media make unhealthy habits like drinking alcohol and smoking look "cool"?

14. What parts of your body do you not have any control over changing? Do you think of those parts as attractive or unattractive?

15. How do you feel when you see someone who is really overweight or underweight?

16. What kind of clothes are you most comfortable in? Why?

From *Girls in Real-Life Situations: Group Counseling Activities for Enhancing Social and Emotional Development—Grades 6–12*
© 2007 by J. V. Taylor and S. Trice-Black. Champaign, IL: Research Press. (800–519–2707, www.researchpress.com)

Body Image (continued)

17. How do you feel in gym class when you must change in front of other people?

18. Do you often compliment other people's looks or their abilities? Why?

19. Do you have a female adult role model in your life you admire, despite her size? What makes her so great?

20. Is it difficult for you to say out loud something you like about your body? Tell the group what you like!

Think about It

Body Image

Directions: Your body is a gift and is the most precious thing you will ever possess. You need to treat it well, nourish it, embrace it, and, most important, accept it! Think about your body and complete the phrases below. Be honest—nobody is looking.

My Body

I like _____

I wish _____

I can change _____

I cannot change _____

I accept _____

I will _____

I am _____

I will try to _____

I will always _____

Below, list all of the important, healthy things your body has done for you.

Optional Journaling Questions

❀ Were your responses mostly positive or negative?

❀ What are you willing to do to keep your body image positive?

❀ Who are the people in your life who love and accept you for who you are, not what you look like?

From *Girls in Real-Life Situations: Group Counseling Activities for Enhancing Social and Emotional Development—Grades 6–12*
© 2007 by J. V. Taylor and S. Trice-Black. Champaign, IL: Research Press. (800–519–2707, www.researchpress.com)

Check It Out

Body Image

Here are some great books for teens. Check them out!

❀ *A Hunger So Wide and So Deep: American Women Speak Out on Eating Problems,* by Becky W. Thompson (Minneapolis: University of Minnesota Press, 1996).

❀ *Over It: A Teen's Guide to Getting Beyond Obsessions with Food and Weight,* by Carol Emery Normandi and Laurelee Roark (Novato, CA: New World Library, 2001).

❀ *Body Talk: The Straight Facts on Fitness, Nutrition, and Feeling Great about Yourself!* by Ann Douglas, Julie Douglas, and Claudia Davila (Ontario, Canada: Maple Tree Press, 2006).

❀ *Real Gorgeous: The Truth about Body and Beauty,* by Kaz Cooke (New York: W.W. Norton, 1996).

❀ *A Look in the Mirror: Freeing Yourself from the Body Image Blues,* by Valerie Rainon McManus (Washington, DC: Child and Family Press, 2004).

From *Girls in Real-Life Situations: Group Counseling Activities for Enhancing Social and Emotional Development—Grades 6–12*
© 2007 by J. V. Taylor and S. Trice-Black. Champaign, IL: Research Press. (800–519–2707, www.researchpress.com)

Choices

Connect!

Choices

Time

10 minutes

Objective

For the girls to explore the importance of making choices in a fun, creative way

Activity

Instruct the girls to imagine that they are going to move to a deserted island. Once they arrive at the island, their food and water will be provided. However, each girl will be given one backpack, in which she can put only five items. These items will be the only items that she can take to the island. Ask each girl to share the five items she would take to the island and to explain her reasoning for choosing each item.

Process Questions

❀ Was it difficult to decide on only five items for your backpack? Explain why or why not.

❀ What are some things that help you make difficult decisions?

❀ Who are some people who help you with your decisions?

Longing to Belong

RATIONALE

Belonging to a group of friends can be wonderful. Friends can give support and help during difficult times. However, at times, being part of a group of friends can be problematic. One negative aspect of being part of a group of friends is pressure to look or act a certain way in order to continue to be a part of the group. People may be willing to do things that go against their beliefs or that they really don't want to do in order to maintain their place in the group. Belonging to a group often helps people feel more secure; in actuality, however, their security should come from within rather than from others. In this activity, the girls will discuss the importance of belonging to a group of friends and understand how it is often OK not to go along with the crowd.

MATERIALS

A copy of the We Belong Together handout for each pair of girls
Pencils or pens

PROCEDURE

1. Pair up the girls.
2. Give each pair a copy of the We Belong Together handout. Have them write down as many things as they can think of that "belong" together.
3. When they are done, begin a discussion about belonging. Ask the girls if sometimes the things they listed don't go together. For example, some people don't enjoy peanut butter with jelly. Ask the girls what they belong to (for example, sports teams, a church group, or a club).
4. Ask the girls what group of friends they belong to. Encourage the girls to talk about the benefits and problems that accompany having a specific group of friends.
5. Ask the girls the following questions:

✿ When are some times that you and your friends don't "go" together? (For example, you might not all play the same sport, ride the same bus, or like the same foods.)

✿ When do you recall doing something with a group of friends that you did not want to do?

✿ Why do you think people sometimes do things that they do not want to do when they are around their friends?

✿ How do you think people act differently when they are around different groups of people?

✿ Why do you think it is difficult for people to say no to their friends?

✿ Where would you draw the line with your friends? In other words, what are some things you would not do?

✿ What are some things that friends sometimes pressure each other to do, to wear, or to say?

✿ Why do you think people continue to be friends with people they are afraid of or who threaten to break off their friendship?

✿ How can you make some healthy choices about your friends when deciding what you are and are not willing to do?

CLOSING QUESTIONS

✿ What was the point of this group session?

✿ What do you think can be done to help girls have healthy friendships with one another?

✿ How will you use what you have learned today in the future?

We Belong Together

Directions: Many things just seem to go together (for example, peanut butter and jelly). Together with your partner, see how many such things you can list!

_____ & _____

_____ & _____

_____ & _____

_____ & _____

_____ & _____

_____ & _____

_____ & _____

_____ & _____

_____ & _____

_____ & _____

From *Girls in Real-Life Situations: Group Counseling Activities for Enhancing Social and Emotional Development—Grades 6–12*
© 2007 by J. V. Taylor and S. Trice-Black. Champaign, IL: Research Press. (800–519–2707, www.researchpress.com)

Risky Business

RATIONALE

When struggling with identity issues and creating a core concept of self, adolescent girls often engage in risky or dangerous behaviors. These behaviors are often choices that result in negative consequences. Unfortunately, girls this age are notorious for believing that "it won't happen to me."

MATERIALS

Copy of any recipe card

Index cards

Pencils or pens

PROCEDURE

1. Ask the girls to define risky or dangerous behaviors and to determine what makes a behavior safe, as opposed to unsafe.
2. Steer the discussion toward these behaviors, as they are undertaken in the context of relationships with girlfriends, boyfriends, family members, and others.
3. Show the girls the recipe card.
4. Explain to the girls how all the ingredients combined together create a specific product, such as a cake or cookies. Explain that if any ingredient or any step in the process is altered, the product will not turn out the way it should.
5. Ask the girls if they have ever left out an ingredient when cooking so that the finished product was less than desirable.
6. Give each girl two index cards and a pen or pencil.
7. Instruct the girls to create their own "recipes." On one index card, the girls should create a recipe describing healthy, productive behaviors. The recipe should include actions and thoughts necessary for promoting healthy behaviors. For example, "Combine 30 minutes of daily exercise, one hour of studying, proper nutrition, being positive, and helping my parents. The results will help me be successful—every day!"

8. On the second index card, the girls should create recipes for risky, unhealthy behaviors. For example, "Eating poorly, not studying, worrying about my family, not getting enough sleep, and watching five hours of TV per day will get me in trouble." Or, for older girls, "Lying to my parents, drinking, staying up until 2 a.m. every night, and skipping school will catch up with me in the long run."

9. When they have finished, have the girls share their recipes and discuss differences and similarities.

10. Have the girls share how they will implement their "recipes for success."

CLOSING QUESTIONS

❀ Can you describe the choices you always have when deciding what risks to take?

❀ When you make an unwise decision, do you often learn from your mistake?

❀ How will you use what you have learned today in the future?

Today I Choose . . .

RATIONALE

Everything we do in life is a choice. Every choice has a consequence. The consequence can be positive or negative. Girls often have a difficult time thinking about the ramifications of their decisions. The pressures and uncertainties during times of trouble can lead to poor choices. This activity focuses on the importance of thinking through and planning to help promote healthy decision making.

MATERIALS

A copy of the My Life Is a Choice handout for each girl

Pencils or pens

PROCEDURE

1. Explain to the girls that they will be focusing on choices. Ask for some examples of the many choices they make every day.

2. Talk about these examples and point out that good choices are often harder to make but usually lead to better results.

3. Talk to the girls about how empowering themselves means to know that most everything they do in life is their choice.

4. Give a copy of the My Life Is a Choice handout to each girl.

5. Have them complete the handout and see how many things they actually choose to do in one day.

6. When the girls are finished, have them talk about a few of their daily choices.

7. When they are done sharing, steer the discussion toward what the consequences may be if they do not make those choices. For example, they may choose to take a shower. If they don't, they will smell bad. Other examples: They choose to brush their teeth. If they don't, they may get cavities. They choose to eat lunch. If they don't, they may get hungry or have a headache.

8. Complete the activity by repeating the idea that making choices is empowering.

CLOSING QUESTIONS

❀ Can you name a few difficult situations in which making a good choice may be a struggle for many girls today?

❀ Why do you think these situations are so difficult?

❀ How would you advise someone to handle these difficult situations?

❀ How will you use what you have learned today in the future?

My Life Is a Choice

Directions: Girls, did you know that most everything you do in life is a choice? You choose to wake up, take a shower, eat breakfast, brush your hair, get dressed, eat, exercise, raise your hand in class, treat your family and friends a certain way, and so on. You make thousands of choices every day! What you are doing right now—IS YOUR CHOICE! Pretty cool, huh? In the space provided, write down all of the choices that you make in one day. Start with hitting that alarm button!

From *Girls in Real-Life Situations: Group Counseling Activities for Enhancing Social and Emotional Development—Grades 6–12*
© 2007 by J. V. Taylor and S. Trice-Black. Champaign, IL: Research Press. (800–519–2707, www.researchpress.com)

Practice What You Preach

RATIONALE

Good decision making is difficult, especially during the teenage years. This activity will help girls focus on common problems encountered by those in their peer group and determine appropriate ways to deal with these problems.

MATERIALS

Paper

Pencils or pens

Clipping from the newspaper of "Dear Abby" or some other advice column

PROCEDURE

1. Show the girls the newspaper clipping of the advice column.
2. Talk about the purpose of an advice column and the reasons that people might want to ask someone for help or advice with a problem.
3. Explain to the girls that each will be creating her own advice column—both the questions and the answers.
4. Let each girl pick a name for her column: "Dear _____."
5. After each girl chooses the name of her column, give her a piece of paper and a pencil or pen.
6. Instruct the girls to write a letter asking for advice about a real or imagined situation that applies to most girls their age.
7. After they have finished, collect all the letters and pass them out in a different order.
8. Have the girls answer the letter that they receive and give helpful advice.
9. After everyone completes her response, each girl will share with the group the letter she received and the advice she offered the writer.

CLOSING QUESTIONS

❀ Which question do you think was the most applicable to girls your age? Explain why.

❀ Which response did you find the most helpful? Explain why.

❀ Who are some people you ask for advice? Why do you ask these people?

❀ How will you use what you have learned today in the future?

Talk about It

Choices

1. How do you make decisions? Do you think about something seemingly forever? Are you impulsive?

2. Talk about the most difficult decision you ever had to make.

3. Talk about the worst decision you ever made.

4. Are you easily influenced by your friends to make decisions you otherwise might not make?

5. Do your friends make decisions for you?

6. How many choices do you make in a day?

7. "Everything you do in life is a choice." What do you think about that quote? Do you believe it to be true?

8. What are some choices you have control over?

9. What are some choices you have no control over?

10. When you believe a friend is making a bad choice, do you confront her and talk about how you feel?

11. Talk about how it feels to hear "I told you so!"

12. If you give a friend advice and she chooses not to follow it, but then it turns out you are right, do you rub it in her face or help her?

13. What are some choices that your parents allow you to make on your own?

14. Do you feel trapped when you have to make a decision?

15. Do you follow your own advice to friends?

16. Has someone ever told you, "You are all talk!"?

17. What are some of the consequences you have had to face for making a wrong choice?

18. Give an example of a time you felt really pressured to do something you felt unsure about.

19. What do you think about the term *peer pressure?*

20. What are some ways you can stay true to yourself and your values when faced with a difficult decision?

From *Girls in Real-Life Situations: Group Counseling Activities for Enhancing Social and Emotional Development—Grades 6–12*
© 2007 by J. V. Taylor and S. Trice-Black. Champaign, IL: Research Press. (800–519–2707, www.researchpress.com)

Think about It

Choices

Sometimes life simply does not go as planned. It is generally the small things in life that upset and anger us the most. What a lot of people fail to realize is that although they have no control in many situations, they have full control over their reactions. YOU ARE ONLY IN CONTROL OF YOU! Overreacting often creates a lot of unnecessary drama. For each situation below, write how you could have a drama-queen reaction, or how you could have a drama-free reaction. Think about how much extra time and head space you may have if you choose to react differently!

1. Your parent was held up at work and was late picking you up from school. Therefore, you were late to your soccer game and had to sit out the first quarter.

    Drama-Queen Reaction:

    Drama-Free Reaction:

2. Your friend was supposed to hang out with you on Friday night. You did not go to the movies with other friends so you could hang out with her. She had to cancel at the last minute because she had to watch her little sister.

    Drama-Queen Reaction:

    Drama-Free Reaction:

From *Girls in Real-Life Situations: Group Counseling Activities for Enhancing Social and Emotional Development—Grades 6–12*
© 2007 by J. V. Taylor and S. Trice-Black. Champaign, IL: Research Press. (800–519–2707, www.researchpress.com)

Choices (continued)

3. You studied really hard for a test and got a C on it. Your friend did not study at all and asked for your notes 10 minutes before the test. She got an A.

   Drama-Queen Reaction:

   Drama-Free Reaction:

4. You spent almost an hour doing your hair this morning, and as soon as you got to school, it started to rain really hard. You were soaked!

   Drama-Queen Reaction:

   Drama-Free Reaction:

5. You made plans to go to the movies on Sunday afternoon with all of your friends. The weather turns out to be beautiful and they decide they want to go to the pool and hang out. You really want to see the movie, but they won't go.

   Drama-Queen Reaction:

   Drama-Free Reaction:

Optional Journaling Questions

❀ Pick one time when you totally freaked out about something small that you had no control over, then write down the situation. Looking back at the situation, write down how you could have reacted differently.

❀ Who are the people in your life that you find it easy to lose control with? Who are the people in your life you would never get upset with? What are the differences in the people? Would some accept your reaction, whereas others wouldn't?

Check It Out

Choices

Here are some great books for teens. Check them out!

❀ *A Teen's Game Plan for Life,* by Lou Holtz (Notre Dame, IN: Sorin Books, 2002).

❀ *Choice Is Yours: A Teenager's Guide to Self-Discovery, Relationships, Values, and Spiritual Growth,* by Bonnie Parsley (New York: Fireside, 1992).

❀ *My Life, My Choices: Key Issues for Young Adults,* by Mary Ann Burkley Wojno (Mahwah, NJ: Paulist Press, 1997).

❀ *The 6 Most Important Decisions You'll Ever Make—A Guide For Teens,* by Sean Covey (New York: Fireside, 2006).

❀ *Am I Weird or Is This Normal? Advice and Info to Get Teens in the Know,* by Marlin S. Potash, Laura Potash Fruitman, and Lisa Sussman (New York: Fireside, 2001).

From *Girls in Real-Life Situations: Group Counseling Activities for Enhancing Social and Emotional Development—Grades 6–12*
© 2007 by J. V. Taylor and S. Trice-Black. Champaign, IL: Research Press. (800–519–2707, www.researchpress.com)

Communication

Communication

Time

10 minutes

Objective

For the girls to explore the importance of nonverbal communication

Materials

Slips of paper, pencils or pens, tape

Preparation

Write the name of a different sport on each slip of paper.

Activity

Tape one slip of paper on the back of each girl. Do not let the girl see what is written on her paper. Instruct the girls to find out what sport is written on their slips of paper without using any verbal communication. The girls must try to tell each other what is written by using only nonverbal communication.

Process Questions

❀ Did you find it difficult to communicate with others without using verbal communication? Explain why or why not.

❀ What types of nonverbal communication most helped you to communicate with others in this activity?

Dealing with Parents

RATIONALE

During the adolescent and teenage years, dealing with parents can be very difficult and prone to conflict. Girls need to be able to ask their parents questions and to talk to them about problems. Too often, conversations between parents and their children are stopped before they even get started. Stressful topics that are presented when people are angry, tired, or feeling hopeless usually provoke fights that do not resolve anything. Girls need to learn appropriate ways and times to approach their parents so they can help open the doors of communication.

MATERIALS

None

PROCEDURE

1. Begin by talking to the girls about the three T's of girl-parent communication: TIME, TALK, and TOPIC.

2. TIME: Pick a time to talk to your parents when people are less likely to be stressed. For example, if you want to go to the dance on Friday night, it is probably best not to ask as soon as your mom or dad walks into the house from work. When you need to talk to your parents about something, make sure you do it—but don't do it when you are already in trouble for something else or when it is late at night.

   Discuss: What are times that are good for you and your parents to talk? What are some times that it is not good for you and your parents to talk? Why do you think time is important?

3. TALK: Talk to your parents. This sounds so simple—but it really isn't! Watch your words and make sure they do not include messages of blame or hurt. It is OK to talk to your parents about how you are feeling, even if that feeling is anger, but make sure that you clearly and calmly present your thoughts and feelings.

Discuss: Talk about some times that you have had success in discussing a difficult situation with your parents. How did you stay calm?

4. TOPIC: When you talk to your parents, stick to the topic! For example, if you want to talk to your parents about a boy, don't go off the topic and start arguing about something else. Remember that it is very difficult for parents and their children to have discussions—but it can be accomplished. Maintain control of the conversation and make sure that you and your parents discuss your topic.

   Discuss: Talk about some topics that are difficult to approach your parents with. Why do you think it is difficult to talk to your parents about these topics? Why do you think people change the subject during a difficult conversation?

CLOSING QUESTIONS

❀ Do you think the three T's would help you in a difficult discussion with your parents?

❀ What are some other tips that you have learned to help you talk to your parents?

❀ How will you use what you have learned today in the future?

Talking It Out

RATIONALE

Conflicts are an inevitable part of everyone's life. Reactions to conflicts can bring peace or can increase anger and possibly even bring about aggression and violence. Girls, like everyone, often have a difficult time resolving conflicts instead of increasing their problems. Having a clear, concrete picture of the conflict can help resolve the problem. Too often, our emotions take over, and the underlying conflict gets clouded over with anger, jealousy, and hurt. In order to help solve problems, we must first identify them. This activity will teach girls to take an objective look at conflicts before attempting to resolve them.

MATERIALS

A copy of the Conflict Analysis handout for each pair of girls
Paper
Pencils or pens

PROCEDURE

1. Begin by discussing the difficulty in resolving conflicts, especially when anger, hurt, rejection, shame, or embarrassment is involved.

2. Pair up the girls and give each pair three sheets of paper and a pencil or pen.

3. Instruct each pair to write down one descriptive example of a common conflict between girls, another between girls and guys, and another between girls and parents.

4. After the girls have completed the descriptive conflicts, collect the papers, mix them up, and redistribute them—one paper per pair. Make sure the girls do not get the same paper they worked on.

5. Instruct each pair to take an objective look at the conflict they read about and complete the Conflict Analysis handout.

6. After they are finished, have each pair share their conflict and their analysis with the other girls.

CLOSING QUESTIONS

❀ Why do you think it is a good idea to clearly identify the facts involved in a conflict before reacting?

❀ Why do you think it is difficult to take a step back and think about a conflict before going with your first reaction?

❀ How will you use what you have learned today in the future?

Conflict Analysis

What is the conflict?

_____

_____

Who is involved in the conflict?

_____

_____

What specific events have happened?

_____

_____

When did the events occur?

_____

_____

Why did the conflict occur?

_____

_____

How could the conflict be prevented?

_____

_____

From *Girls in Real-Life Situations: Group Counseling Activities for Enhancing Social and Emotional Development—Grades 6–12*
© 2007 by J. V. Taylor and S. Trice-Black. Champaign, IL: Research Press. (800–519–2707, www.researchpress.com)

Body Language

RATIONALE

We constantly communicate with others through our body language. Without uttering a single word, we are able to convey messages of anger, sadness, fear, excitement, hope, embarrassment—and the list goes on and on! People are often unaware of the signals they are sending to others simply by crossing their arms, clenching their fists, turning their heads, or looking down. It is important for girls to be aware of the messages that their own bodies are sending to others through nonverbal communication as well as the body language of others. In this activity, the girls will identify different feelings associated with body language.

MATERIALS

Paper

Pencils or pens

PROCEDURE

1. Begin by talking to the girls about the importance of body language.

2. Demonstrate different examples of body language and let the girls name the emotion that is being portrayed. For example, cross your arms or wrinkle your brow and frown for anger, look down at the floor for sadness or embarrassment, or roll your eyes for disrespect.

3. Discuss the importance of noticing the body language of others as well as paying attention to the messages that your body is sending to other people.

4. Pair up the girls and give each pair a piece of paper and a pen or pencil.

5. Instruct each pair to write a short skit involving a conflict or a situation involving two or more emotions. Don't tell them they will be performing the skit without words.

6. After the girls have finished their skits, have each pair act out their skit in front of the group—WITHOUT words!

7. See if the group can guess the emotions portrayed through the girls' body language.

CLOSING QUESTIONS

❀ What type of body language easily reveals someone's emotions?

❀ Can you recall certain occasions when you might not be aware of how your body is reacting to the way you are feeling? What are they?

❀ How will you use what you have learned today in the future?

Social Graces

RATIONALE

Manners are an important part of our daily lives. Unfortunately, many people today do not get the opportunity to learn and practice good manners. This activity allows girls to learn and practice good manners and appropriate social skills in a fun, relaxed way.

MATERIALS

Teacups and saucers

Teakettle or pitcher filled with lemonade, tea, or punch

Cookies or crackers

Plates and napkins

CD player and a CD of classical music

Table and chairs

A name tag for each girl

PROCEDURE

1. Before the meeting, set the table properly and assign seats using name tags.
2. Begin this activity by explaining to the girls that today they have been invited to a fancy tea party. (If possible, tell them a few days before the group and invite them to dress up.)
3. Explain to them that during this tea party, quiet, classical music will be played.
4. Tell the girls that they will need to use their best manners.
5. Seat each girl at the table, instructing each one to say thank you and quietly sit in her seat.
6. Instruct the girls to place their napkins in their laps.
7. Ask the girls if anyone would like some tea or lemonade or punch.

8. Instruct the girls on appropriate ways to respond when offered something to drink.

9. Demonstrate how the tea should be poured and how the pitcher should be passed from one person to the next around the table.

10. Praise the girls for their patience in waiting their turn and for their excellent manners. Pass the crackers or cookies around in the same manner.

11. Encourage the girls to have an appropriate mealtime discussion in quiet voices. Suggest they discuss "safe" subjects, such as their interests and hobbies.

12. Continue to praise the girls for appropriate behaviors.

13. Even though there may be some giggling during this activity, the girls will probably get into the idea of the "fancy" tea party and the importance of using their best manners.

14. When they are finished, instruct them on how to clean up properly and remind them to thank you for being the "host" of a fabulous party!

CLOSING QUESTIONS

❀ How did it feel to sit at the table during the tea party?

❀ Why do you think it is important for people to use good manners?

❀ How will you use what you have learned today in the future?

Talk about It

Communication

1. Whom do you have the most trouble communicating with? What makes it so difficult?
2. Have you ever been with someone who had horrible manners? What was it like?
3. How do you react when someone is rude to a stranger?
4. How important do you think body language is while having a discussion?
5. Do you find it easy or difficult to talk to someone you don't know?
6. What is something you wish you could talk to your parents about?
7. When you are having a conflict with someone, do you go directly to the person, or do you think about it first?
8. Can you talk about a time you got really angry and went off on someone and later regretted it?
9. Have you ever lied to your parents to get out of trouble?
10. Have you ever been caught lying and lost the trust of someone you care about?
11. Can you talk about a time you felt really hurt by miscommunication?
12. When you get your feelings hurt, do you find it easier to talk about it or just to let it slide?
13. How have e-mail, text messaging, and the Internet made communication easier?
14. Do you think we are getting less personal because of technology?
15. What is something you have written using instant messaging or e-mail that you have later regretted?
16. How would you rate your manners on a scale of 1 to 10?
17. Is there a difference between how you treat your friends' parents and how you treat your own?
18. What is one thing about your communication style that you think you need to improve?
19. What communication style are you most comfortable with? For example, some people do not like to talk on the phone.
20. When do you think it is appropriate to confront somebody you are upset with?

From *Girls in Real-Life Situations: Group Counseling Activities for Enhancing Social and Emotional Development—Grades 6–12*
© 2007 by J. V. Taylor and S. Trice-Black. Champaign, IL: Research Press. (800–519–2707, www.researchpress.com)

Think about It

Communication

Friends

I'd like to talk to my friends about _____

_____

_____

I wish I could explain to my friends that _____

_____

_____

Parents

I wish I could ask my parent about _____

_____

_____

I wish my parent understood that _____

_____

_____

Time, Talk, Topic

I am going to talk to my parent about _____

The time I am going to talk to them is _____

From *Girls in Real-Life Situations: Group Counseling Activities for Enhancing Social and Emotional Development—Grades 6–12*
© 2007 by J. V. Taylor and S. Trice-Black. Champaign, IL: Research Press. (800–519–2707, www.researchpress.com)

Communication (continued)

One way I am going to make sure I stay calm is _____

_____

Another adult I can talk to is _____

Optional Journaling Questions

❀ When talking about problems, what makes it difficult for you to open up?

❀ What are some of the things you have trouble talking about?

Check It Out

Communication

Here are some great books for teens. Check them out!

❈ *How Rude! The Teenagers' Guide to Good Manners, Proper Behavior, and Not Grossing People Out,* by Alex J. Packer (Minneapolis: Free Spirit Publishing, 1997).

❈ *Bringing Up Parents: The Teenager's Handbook,* by Alex J. Packer, Pamela Espeland, and Harry Pulver (Minneapolis: Free Spirit Publishing, 1992).

❈ *GirlWise: How to Be Confident, Capable, Cool, and in Control,* by Julia Devillers (New York: Three Rivers Press, 2002).

❈ *Life Lists for Teens: Tips, Steps, Hints, and How-Tos for Growing Up, Getting Along, Learning, and Having Fun,* by Pamela Espeland (Minneapolis: Free Spirit Publishing, 2003).

❈ *Life Strategies for Teens,* by Jay McGraw (New York: Fireside, 2004).

From *Girls in Real-Life Situations: Group Counseling Activities for Enhancing Social and Emotional Development—Grades 6–12*
© 2007 by J. V. Taylor and S. Trice-Black. Champaign, IL: Research Press. (800–519–2707, www.researchpress.com)

Emotions

Connect!

Emotions

Time

10 minutes

Objective

To help girls understand the wide array of emotions they feel daily

Materials

None

Activity

Call out the first letter of the alphabet. When the girls hear it, someone should yell out a feeling that corresponds with the letter. For example, if you call out *A!* one of the girls may say "anger" or "anxiety." Together, the group then demonstrates whatever feeling was called out. Repeat this process through the entire alphabet once or twice.

Process Questions

❀ How many different emotions were called out that you feel on a regular basis?

❀ Do you have trouble communicating those emotions, or is it easier to say you are just fine, regardless? Why or why not?

The Boiling Point

RATIONALE

For most adolescents, the teen years are filled with erratic episodes of anger and extreme moodiness. When girls get angry, they often displace their anger. They either internalize it or take it out on someone undeserving of an outburst. Recognizing their anger and how to deal with it appropriately can greatly help teens navigate these roller-coaster years. This activity allows each girl to recognize her "boiling point" and to use anger-management techniques that are unique and useful to her.

MATERIALS

A copy of My Boiling Point for each girl

Pencils or pens

PROCEDURE

1. Tell the girls that today they will be discussing anger.
2. Ask the girls how to cook something that requires boiling, such as pasta or rice.
3. If they do not give a thorough explanation, elaborate by explaining that water would be placed in the pot, the pot would then be placed on the stove (on high heat), and the water would need to boil before pasta or rice could be added to it.
4. Ask the girls questions about how they can determine that water is boiling.

    Example: What are the signs that the water is getting hot, that it is getting ready to boil, and that it is finally boiling? Answers such as "feeling the heat coming from the water," "seeing and feeling steam," "noticing bubbles forming in the water" can be explored with the girls. Talk about what can happen if the pot contains too much water—that there is the possibility that the water will boil over.

5. Encourage the girls to talk about how our anger and tempers are similar to boiling water.

6. Ask, "What can happen if we start to boil? What happens if we boil over?"

7. Ask, "What are signs that our anger is beginning or that we are getting ready to lose our temper (like the steam or bubbles for the boiling water)?"

8. After the group discusses anger, losing tempers, and how to tell that anger is building, hand out a copy of My Boiling Point to each girl.

9. Instruct the girls to list along the thermometer those things that make them angry and to list on the clipboard those things that cool them off.

10. After they are finished, have the group members share their thermometers and clipboards with one another.

CLOSING QUESTIONS

❀ Is it OK to get angry?

❀ What did you learn today about your anger?

❀ How will you use what you have learned today in the future?

My Boiling Point

Directions: Along the right side of the thermometer, list the things that make you angry. On the clipboard, list the things that help you cool off.

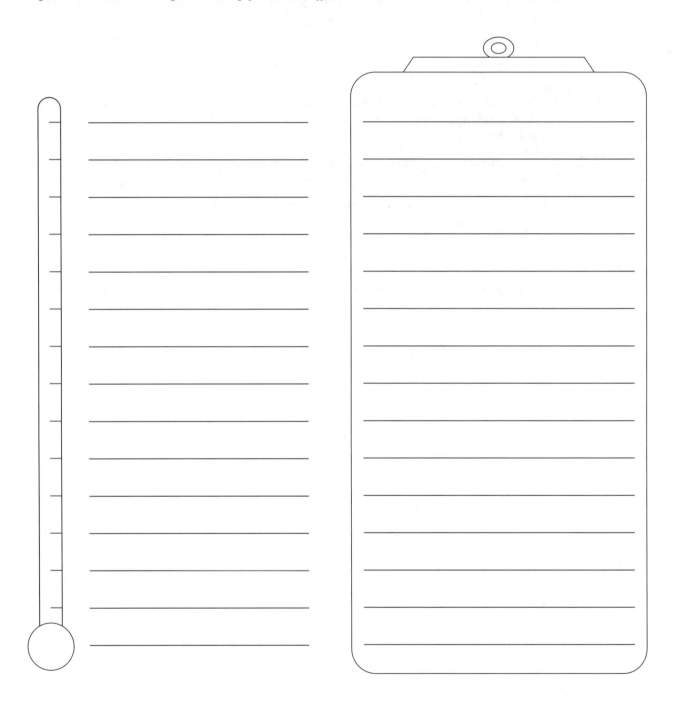

From *Girls in Real-Life Situations: Group Counseling Activities for Enhancing Social and Emotional Development—Grades 6–12*
© 2007 by J. V. Taylor and S. Trice-Black. Champaign, IL: Research Press. (800–519–2707, www.researchpress.com)

Pandora's Box

RATIONALE

Jealousy and envy often cause problems between friends. Adolescents in particular struggle with being satisfied with such things as their appearance, their clothes, and their possessions, and their friends often are jealous of what they believe their friends have. When jealousy and envy enter into relationships, they can result in hurt, anger, and lost friendships. This activity aims at improving self-satisfaction and reducing jealousy and envy.

MATERIALS

Paper

Pencils or pens

Magazines and scissors

A shoe box

Tape

PROCEDURE

1. Begin the group session by briefly telling the story of Pandora's box. A brief summary of the story follows:

   > Greek mythology includes the story of Pandora, a beautiful woman who wanted or needed nothing. Pandora became curious about the possessions locked inside a box. Instead of being satisfied with her own life, Pandora let her curiosity about the box take over. Unable to withstand her curiosity, Pandora opened the box and took a peek inside. Unwittingly, she also released the contents of the box—a multitude of evil powers that spread throughout the world.

2. Ask the girls for their reactions to the story they've just heard.

3. Next, discuss the meaning of the word *satisfied.* Encourage the girls to talk about things they want that they don't have—things

that cause them to be jealous or envious of others. Discuss the meanings of the words *envy* and *jealousy* and talk about the problems that these two emotions can cause in relationships.

4. Explain to the group that they are going to create their own Pandora's Box. This box will contain pictures, symbols, and descriptions of things that cause jealousy and envy in relationships.

5. Hand out the materials.

6. Instruct the girls to write descriptions of problems, cut photographs out of magazines of things that can trigger jealousy or envy, or draw pictures related to this topic.

7. Allow each girl the opportunity to share her creation with the group and to explain how it causes problems and how these problems can be prevented.

8. After they share their creations, have the girls place their drawings, writings, or magazine photographs in the box.

9. After everyone has had a turn, close the box and seal it with tape.

10. Explain that this box now contains the girls' feelings of jealousy and envy and that it is sealed.

11. Discuss the symbolic meaning of sealing up and putting away the problems of jealousy and envy.

CLOSING QUESTIONS

❀ How do you think your relationships with your friends would improve if jealousy and envy were not factors?

❀ Why do you think people have a difficult time being satisfied with what they have?

❀ How will you use what you have learned today in the future?

The Blame Game

RATIONALE

Adolescents often blame other people for their problems and assume that everyone is out to ruin their lives. Most have trouble accepting responsibility for their actions. They often believe that adults should be able to read their minds and have trouble asking for help. Blaming only leads to more conflicts. Statements including the words *always* and *never,* as well as statements like "Nobody understands" and "It is their entire fault," are examples of blaming statements that prevent people from taking responsibility for their actions or seeking help when facing difficulty. In this activity, the girls will play The Blame Game and become aware of the amount of blaming they do.

MATERIALS

Small ball

Basket or bowl

Copy of The Blame Game Statements (cut into slips and placed in the basket or bowl)

PROCEDURE

1. Prior to the group meeting, place the slips with the blaming phrases in the bowl or basket.

2. Have the girls sit in a circle or around a table.

3. Begin the group with a discussion about blaming. Ask the girls to give examples of how easy it is to blame other people for our mistakes.

4. Talk about the statement "It's not my fault!" Ask the girls about the last time they said it.

5. Pass the basket or bowl to each girl and instruct her to close her eyes and pick out one of the phrases.

6. Have each girl read aloud the blaming statement she selected and instruct the group to discuss briefly how this statement can be

used to avoid responsibility and how it can result in relationship problems.

7. After each girl has had a turn, give the instructions for The Blame Game:

In this game, a small ball will passed around the circle. As soon as someone receives the ball, she has 10 seconds in which to use a blaming statement. If she repeats a statement that was previously used in the game or takes longer than 10 seconds, she must take part in a "confessional," in which she has to talk about one of the following: a time that blaming caused her difficulties, ways to prevent blaming, or problems that can result from blaming. When she's finished, the game resumes by having her pass the ball to the next person.

8. Continue until group time is up.

CLOSING QUESTIONS

❀ What makes it difficult to accept responsibility for your actions?

❀ What feelings do people avoid when they constantly blame other people for their actions?

❀ How will you use what you have learned today in the future?

The Blame Game Statements

It's not my fault!	It's your fault we got in trouble!
She started it!	If you listened to me, everything would be fine!
He made me do it!	Why did you make me do that?
I can't help it!	You ruined EVERYTHING!
It's my mom's fault that I am late!	You NEVER listen to me!
How come she got away with it last week?	You are SO lazy!
You don't care about me!	We lost the game because of her!

From *Girls in Real-Life Situations: Group Counseling Activities for Enhancing Social and Emotional Development—Grades 6–12*
© 2007 by J. V. Taylor and S. Trice-Black. Champaign, IL: Research Press. (800–519–2707, www.researchpress.com)

Feeling Blue

RATIONALE

Feelings are often difficult for adolescents to understand and discuss. Sadness, in particular, can be difficult for adolescents to talk about because of their natural need to protect themselves. This activity provides a safe venue for the girls in the group to discuss their feelings of sadness, the events and circumstances that may provoke sadness in them, and the various techniques they use to process these feelings.

MATERIALS

Colored markers, paint, markers, and pastels in different shades of blue

Drawing paper

CD player and a CD of soft, mellow music

PROCEDURE

1. Ask the girls about the feeling of sadness. Encourage them to talk about times when they are sad, how they know others are sad, and what events make people sad.

2. Ask the girls about "feeling blue." Why do people associate sadness with the color blue?

3. Pass the markers, paint, and pastels around the group. Encourage the girls to talk about what these different shades of blue make them think about and feel.

4. Tell the girls that they will be using these shades of blue to create a picture or design about sadness.

5. Give each girl a piece of blank paper and play the soft, mellow music while the girls work on their pictures.

6. When all the girls are finished with their pictures, invite each one to share her work with the group.

CLOSING QUESTIONS

❀ What are some ways you express yourself when you feel sad? For example, do you get angry? Do you cry? Do you sleep?

❀ How will you use what you have learned today in the future?

Talk about It

Emotions

1. Talk about a time you recall when a minor situation caused you to lose your temper.
2. Do you consider yourself an emotional person? Why or why not?
3. What are some unhealthy ways that you express your emotions?
4. Why do you think that girls are so emotional?
5. Do you control anger, or does anger control you?
6. Whom do you get angry at the most?
7. Whom do you take your anger out on?
8. Have you ever seen people get violent when they are angry?
9. Talk about a time when you were overemotional and later regretted it.
10. How do your family members express their emotions?
11. Has anyone ever called you a "drama queen?" If so, how did you feel about it?
12. Do you ever feel that your parents ignore your feelings?
13. What are some situations that really make you emotional?
14. Name some of the emotions or feelings that are typical of you every day.
15. When do you feel the most emotional?
16. What is the worst thing you have done while you were angry with someone?
17. Talk about a time when you regretted being overemotional.
18. In what situations do you wish you could be more relaxed?
19. When have you witnessed people out of control when they were angry?
20. What are some healthy ways for you to express your emotions?

From *Girls in Real-Life Situations: Group Counseling Activities for Enhancing Social and Emotional Development—Grades 6–12*
© 2007 by J. V. Taylor and S. Trice-Black. Champaign, IL: Research Press. (800–519–2707, www.researchpress.com)

Think about It

Emotions

Directions: Think about your anger. What does it look like? How do you express it? Would you be open to changing how you express your anger? Think about it below and honestly finish the statements.

1. When I get angry, I . . .

   Is my reaction healthy? Why or why not?

2. How does my family express their anger? (List each family member who lives in your house and describe what he or she does when angry.)

   Are my family's reactions healthy? Why or why not?

3. Some healthy alternative ways I can handle my anger are . . .

4. The people I can talk to when I get angry are . . .

Optional Journaling Questions

❀ When was the last time you got really mad at someone and directed your anger at him or her?

❀ Why do you think it is easier to blame other people than to accept responsibility when you get mad?

From *Girls in Real-Life Situations: Group Counseling Activities for Enhancing Social and Emotional Development—Grades 6–12*
© 2007 by J. V. Taylor and S. Trice-Black. Champaign, IL: Research Press. (800–519–2707, www.researchpress.com)

Check It Out

Emotions

Here are some great books for teens. Check them out!

❀ *Respect: A Girl's Guide to Getting Respect and Dealing When Your Line Is Crossed,* by Courtney Macavinta and Andrea Vander Pluym (Minneapolis: Free Spirit Publishing, 2005).

❀ *My Feelings Are Like Wild Animals: How Do I Tame Them? A Practical Guide to Help Teens (and Former Teens) Feel and Deal with Painful Emotions,* by Gary Egeberg (Mahwah, NJ: Paulist Press, 1998).

❀ *Happiness Is a Choice for Teens,* by Paul Meier (Nashville: Thomas Nelson, 1996).

❀ *Girl to Girl: Daily Thoughts on Living for Girls Ages 11–15,* by Karen Casey (Center City, MN: Hazleden, 2000).

❀ *How to Take the GRRRR Out of Anger,* by Elizabeth Verdick and Marjorie Lisovskis (Minneapolis: Free Spirit Publishing, 2002).

From *Girls in Real-Life Situations: Group Counseling Activities for Enhancing Social and Emotional Development—Grades 6–12*
© 2007 by J. V. Taylor and S. Trice-Black. Champaign, IL: Research Press. (800–519–2707, www.researchpress.com)

Friendships

Connect!

Friendships

Time

10 minutes

Objective

To help the girls discuss positive and negative aspects of friendships

Materials

Magazine picture or photo of two or more girls together

Activity

Instruct the girls to sit in a circle. Show the picture to the girls and explain that the group will tell a story about the friendship of the girls in the picture. Each girl says a few sentences about the picture, and then the next girl continues the story. For example, you may begin by saying to the first girl, "These girls are getting ready to go to a movie. They are deciding what to wear." The next girl adds a few sentences, and the process continues until everyone in the circle has had a turn. After five minutes or so, end the story and encourage the girls to discuss it.

Process Questions

❀ What were some of the positive characteristics of friendship described in the group's story?

❀ What were some of the negative characteristics that were described?

❀ How might different people view or interpret the same situation in different ways?

Mean Teens

RATIONALE

Gossiping, spreading rumors, excluding others, backstabbing, using put-downs, and exposing secrets are all forms of aggression that girls use to hurt and manipulate each other. By developing new social skills, girls are better able to empathize with others and consider the impact their actions have on others. Social skills that are not focused on self, but rather on the needs of others, help make our society and world a more peaceful, enjoyable, accepting place. This activity is designed to help girls think about everyday situations from another person's point of view.

MATERIALS

A pair of dice

Relational Aggression Examples (photocopied and cut apart)

Small bowl, basket, cup, hat, or similar container

PROCEDURE

1. Have the girls sit in a circle.
2. Ask the girls what they know about relational aggression (RA). Chances are they don't know much, so explain to them that RA means using friendships, as opposed to fists or weapons, to get what you want.
3. Read the RA statements to the group, one by one. As you read them, ask the girls to talk about each word and how it sometimes represents a problematic situation.
4. Explain to the girls that they will be participating in a game where they will need to think about the feelings of people who are on the receiving end of one of these problems.

Game Directions

Place the RA statements in the bowl. Have one girl select a slip of paper and roll the dice. If she rolls an odd number, she must give an example of a time that the problem on her paper has affected her and how she felt. If she rolls an even number, the girl on her left must give an example. If she rolls doubles, the topic is up to the group to discuss for a few minutes—to share feelings and experiences that resulted from this problem. After the first girl completes her turn, have the girl to her right take her turn in the same manner. Continue playing until each girl has taken a turn.

CLOSING QUESTIONS

❀ What are some of the feelings that these problems seem to bring about?

❀ Why do you think girls are relationally aggressive to one another? What can you do to help prevent this type of aggression from happening?

❀ How will you use what you have learned today in the future?

Relational Aggression Examples

Backstabbing	Revealing secrets
Spreading rumors	Making fun of someone's weight behind her back
Gossiping	Using friends to gain social status
Being sarcastic	Using put-downs
Rolling your eyes	Calling someone a nasty name
Isolating someone	Prank calling
Taunting someone	Laughing
Bumping into someone on purpose	Stealing someone's boyfriend

From *Girls in Real-Life Situations: Group Counseling Activities for Enhancing Social and Emotional Development—Grades 6–12*
© 2007 by J. V. Taylor and S. Trice-Black. Champaign, IL: Research Press. (800–519–2707, www.researchpress.com)

The Social Jungle

RATIONALE

Many girls say it is important to be popular. In times of transition (for example, elementary school to middle school, middle school to high school), friendships may be particularly difficult for girls because of the changing social scene. Girls may trade in "true" friends, whom they can identify with and trust, for "new" friends, who are popular and well liked. In trying to navigate a more popular social circle, they often end up hurt. In this activity, the girls will explore the meaning of friendship, what being and having a true friend entails, and the different ways one can be a true friend.

MATERIALS

  A copy of The Friendship Deed of Trust for each girl

  Pens or pencils

  Scrap paper

  Easel pad or whiteboard

PROCEDURE

1. On the easel pad or whiteboard, write the quote "To have a friend, you must be a friend."
2. Tell the girls to study the quote for two minutes without talking. When the two minutes are up, invite the girls to share what they think the quote means.
3. After discussion, ask the girls to brainstorm the different cliques in their school.
4. Select one girl to record the names of the cliques on scrap paper. Some examples of cliques might be drama geeks, band geeks, gothic chicks, nerds, loners, cheerleaders, jocks, lesbians, floaters, and bangers (names change daily, and the girls should have no problem coming up with a long list). When the list is complete, ask the girls the following questions:

❊ Which one of these groups do you most identify with?

❊ Which one would you want to be friends with?

❊ Which one would you never be friends with?

❊ Which one do you wish you were like?

5. After the girls have answered the questions, ask them the following:

❊ How do you become friends with someone?

❊ How do you know if you are true friends with her?

6. Hand each girl a copy of The Friendship Deed of Trust and have the girls list the qualities they expect and seek in a real friend. Discuss these individual qualities.

7. Begin another discussion about what to do when a friendship goes awry. Have the girls come up with both a positive and a negative way to deal with the following situations.

Situation 1

Your friend invites you to the movies after school and then tells you, at the last minute, that she can't go. You decide to go to the mall anyhow and see your friend with other girls.

Situation 2

Your friend tells you not to like a guy because he is "so wrong for you." You trust her and give him up, only to find out that she really likes him and is going to ask him out.

Situation 3

Your friend asks you if she can copy your homework. You are afraid that you are going to get caught, plus you're annoyed because you worked really hard on it!

Situation 4

Your two friends are fighting, and one of them asks you to "pretend you are mad at her" to get the other friend to talk about her. She wants you then to come and tell her everything.

Situation 5

Your friend is smothering you. She is everywhere you are and gets upset when you hang out with other people, when you can't go over to her house, and even when you are not at your computer when she instant messages you.

CLOSING QUESTIONS

❀ What is the most important thing you learned about yourself today?

❀ At the beginning of the group, we discussed the quote "To have a friend, you must be a friend." Does this statement mean anything different to you now?

❀ How will you use what you have learned today in the future?

The Friendship Deed of Trust

Directions: Write down the qualities that you give and expect in a true friendship. For example: Real friends help each other with their problems; real friends are always there for each other. Then list what real friends don't do: Real friends don't tell secrets about each other unless they think they are in danger; real friends don't talk behind each other's back.

REAL FRIENDS DO:

_____

_____

_____

_____

_____

REAL FRIENDS DON'T:

_____

_____

_____

_____

_____

From *Girls in Real-Life Situations: Group Counseling Activities for Enhancing Social and Emotional Development—Grades 6–12*
© 2007 by J. V. Taylor and S. Trice-Black. Champaign, IL: Research Press. (800–519–2707, www.researchpress.com)

Showdown!

RATIONALE

Conflicts are part of everyday life. Unfortunately, conflicts during the middle school years, for girls especially, can take over friendships and monopolize much of girls' time. This activity helps girls focus on what some of the common conflicts are that girls face at this age and suggests ways they can help prevent these conflicts from ruining their friendships.

MATERIALS

Basket or hat

Slips of paper

Pencils or pens

A copy of the Showdown Skit handout for each pair of girls

PROCEDURE

1. Begin the group by asking the girls to share some of the common conflicts they face with their friends.

2. As the girls mention different conflicts, write them on the slips of paper.

3. After the girls have come up with seven conflicts, have them discuss the various causes of these conflicts, plus the ways they can be addressed and prevented.

4. Place the slips of paper inside the hat or basket, divide the girls into pairs, and have each pair pick one conflict from the hat or basket.

5. Give a copy of the Showdown Skit handout to each pair of girls.

6. Instruct each pair to create and perform a role play that depicts the conflict and shows a way to deal with it.

7. After all the pairs have completed their role plays, have the group discuss the activity.

CLOSING QUESTIONS

❀ Which of the ways suggested to deal with the conflicts do you think would work in a real-life situation?

❀ Why is it so difficult to make good decisions when you are dealing with a conflict?

❀ How will you use what you have learned today in the future?

Showdown Skit

Directions: In the space provided, make up a short skit about the conflict you chose. The skit can be based on a real incident, or it may be about a situation you often see. Here is your chance to shine! Be as creative and specific as you can and remember to try to come up with a positive ending.

_____

_____

_____

_____

_____

_____

_____

_____

_____

_____

_____

_____

_____

From *Girls in Real-Life Situations: Group Counseling Activities for Enhancing Social and Emotional Development—Grades 6–12*
© 2007 by J. V. Taylor and S. Trice-Black. Champaign, IL: Research Press. (800–519–2707, www.researchpress.com)

The Silent Treatment

RATIONALE

In dealing with one another, girls often use silence aggressively. Adults may underestimate how hurtful and cruel silence can be when girls decide to alienate one girl from everyone else. Alienation and isolation are unacceptable behaviors and are considered to be forms of bullying. This activity will help the girls see the importance of including everyone and provide them with the tools needed to combat the silent treatment.

MATERIALS

A large piece of posterboard or butcher paper
Colored markers

PROCEDURE

1. Give all the girls, except for one, a colored marker.
2. Invite everyone who has a marker to decorate the paper or poster-board, creating a banner for the G.I.R.L.S. group.
3. Instruct the girl without a marker to ask you whether she can have one. When she does, reply, "No, not now."
4. After a few minutes, have all the girls stop and ask them whether they noticed anything unusual about the activity. One or more girls will most likely mention that the one girl was not given a marker to participate in the activity.
5. Ask the girl who was not included in the activity how she felt about being left out.
6. Explain to the girl and to the other group members that this is exactly what the activity is trying to show—what it is like when one person is not included.
7. Explain to the group that you did not pick this girl for any particular reason—that she was selected purely at random—and that she will be free to finish making the banner with the rest of the group after the discussion.

8. Ask whether everyone in the group noticed that the girl was left out of the activity.

9. Talk about some things the rest of the group could have done to help include the girl during this activity (for example, share markers).

10. Ask the girl what she could have done instead of just sitting there and waiting.

11. Ask the girl if, once she realized she was being left out, she could have done something else (for example, talked to you or looked at a book).

12. Talk to the girls about the ways this activity carries over into real-life situations.

    ❀ Ask them to talk about times they have been left out.

    ❀ Ask them to confess to a time they purposely excluded another girl and made her well aware of it.

13. Encourage the girls to share what they did to help them feel better during those times they were left out. Ask if they discovered any new activities or new friends in the process.

14. Remind the girls that they do not need to be friends with everyone or like everyone or invite everyone to their parties—but that they do have to respect everyone.

15. After discussion, give the "left out" girl a marker and ask all the girls to decorate the banner. Encourage them to decorate the banner with words or drawings that indicate friendship skills, tips, and ways to include everyone.

CLOSING QUESTIONS

❀ Why do you think girls sometimes exclude someone?

❀ How do you think it feels to be the one who is left out?

❀ How will you use what you have learned today in the future?

Talk about It

Friendships

1. How do girlfriends differ from boyfriends?
2. Talk about your favorite memory of doing something with a girlfriend.
3. What are some ways that girls are mean to one another?
4. Talk about the meanest thing you ever did to a friend.
5. Talk about feeling intimidated by other girls.
6. When is a time you spread a rumor about a friend?
7. Is it important for you to be popular?
8. Do you consider yourself a peacemaker among your friends?
9. Have you ever purposely excluded a friend? Why did you do it?
10. If you are mean to someone, how do you justify it?
11. When was a time you felt vengeful and acted out that way?
12. When you witness girls being aggressive to one another, do you intervene? Why or why not?
13. What is the best thing about girl friendships?
14. How do you make and keep friends?
15. What is relational aggression? Does it happen to you?
16. Have you ever lost a good friend? Why or how?
17. Do you consider yourself a good friend?
18. What are some ways that you stick up for your friends?
19. Is it better to have a few close friends or a lot of acquaintances?
20. How can girls stick together and break the cycle of relational aggression?

From *Girls in Real-Life Situations: Group Counseling Activities for Enhancing Social and Emotional Development—Grades 6–12*
© 2007 by J. V. Taylor and S. Trice-Black. Champaign, IL: Research Press. (800–519–2707, www.researchpress.com)

Think about It

Friendships

❋ Have you ever seen a product that you thought was going to be really cool, but then were disappointed when you used it?

❋ Have you ever been to the grocery store and bought a food item that you thought was going to be really good because of the way it was packaged, but once you opened the package, you thought it was gross?

❋ Have you ever seen a commercial for a medication that promises to make your life better, but at the end lists a ton of side effects?

For this exercise, you will make a personal commercial about yourself. Write a paragraph about why someone would want to be friends with you. Say what is so awesome about you that the person should be friends with you. For example:

I am a good listener, funny, organized, have a great sense of humor, am nice, love to shop, have a cool bedroom, am good at sports, and am fun to go to the movies with. In addition, my parents take me anywhere.

Write your answer here:

_____

_____

_____

_____

_____

_____

_____

From *Girls in Real-Life Situations: Group Counseling Activities for Enhancing Social and Emotional Development—Grades 6–12*
© 2007 by J. V. Taylor and S. Trice-Black. Champaign, IL: Research Press. (800–519–2707, www.researchpress.com)

Friendships (continued)

Now write down the "fine print." This means that you have to be honest and include the not-so-nice parts about you that you may need to work on to make more lasting friendships. The fine print might look something like this:

> I sometimes tell secrets; I like to be the center of attention; I don't like it when my friends hang out without me, but I hang out with other people without them.

Write your fine print here:

_____

_____

_____

What did you learn from this activity?

_____

_____

_____

How can you use what you have learned to improve your friendships?

_____

_____

_____

Optional Journaling Questions
❀ What qualities do you always offer in a friendship?
❀ Why do your friends like you?

Check It Out

Friendships

Here are some great books for teens. Check them out!

❀ *A Smart Girl's Guide to Friendship Troubles,* by Patti Kelley Criswell and Angela Martini (Middleton, WI: Pleasant Company Publications, 2005).

❀ *Best Friends: The Pleasures and Perils of Girls' and Women's Friendships,* by Terri Apter and Ruthellen Josselson (New York: Three Rivers Press, 1999). *Note: This book is better for high schoolage girls.*

❀ *Mean Chicks, Cliques, and Dirty Tricks: A Real Girl's Guide to Getting through the Day with Smarts and Style,* by Erika V. Shearin Karres (Avon, MA: Adams Media, 2004).

❀ *Odd Girl Speaks Out: Girls Write about Bullies, Cliques, Popularity, and Jealousy,* by Rachel Simmons (Orlando, FL: Harcourt, 2002).

❀ *How to Win Friends and Influence People for Teen Girls,* by Donna Dale Carnegie (New York: Fireside, 2005).

From *Girls in Real-Life Situations: Group Counseling Activities for Enhancing Social and Emotional Development—Grades 6–12*
© 2007 by J. V. Taylor and S. Trice-Black. Champaign, IL: Research Press. (800–519–2707, www.researchpress.com)

Relationships

Connect!

Relationships

Time

10 minutes

Objective

To help the girls explore positive characteristics of healthy relationships

Materials

A small ball

Activity

Instruct the girls to stand up and take turns tossing the ball to one another. After catching the ball, each girl must yell out a positive characteristic of a healthy relationship, such as "fun" or "loyal." If a girl drops the ball or takes more than five seconds to answer, she is "out" and must be seated until the next round begins.

Process Questions

❀ What are your favorite characteristics—ones that you heard during the game?

❀ What characteristics do you think are difficult to find in relationships today?

Guy World

RATIONALE

When girls describe "the perfect girl," they typically say she has "the perfect boyfriend." This assumption creates undue pressure on girls to have a boyfriend, even though they may not really want one. This activity allows girls to explore whether they are ready to have a boyfriend, or if they just *think* they should have one.

MATERIALS

A copy of the To Date or Not to Date handout for each girl

Pencils or pens

PROCEDURE

1. Begin the group by asking the girls to describe "the perfect girl." When they mention "the perfect girl's boyfriend," ask them to describe him.

2. Ask the girls to talk about themselves in relation to the boys they have dated or "gone out with." What attracted them to one another? How long did the relationship last? Did they see each other outside of school? Did each girl feel pressure from her friends to go out with the boy? If any of the girls was seeing a boy for a while and then stopped, why did she break up with him?

3. Tell the girls they are going to take a quiz and discuss their personal readiness for relationships.

4. Give each girl a copy of the To Date or Not to Date handout. Allow them a few minutes to complete the quiz.

5. When they are finished, invite each girl to share her results with the group.

6. Discuss the qualities the girls seek in a relationship and what is important to them versus what is important to their friends.

CLOSING QUESTIONS

❀ Do you agree with the results of your quiz? Why or why not?

❀ Is it important to have a boyfriend?

❀ How will you use what you have learned today in the future?

To Date or Not to Date

Directions: Circle the letter that best describes how you would respond to the following questions.

1. I want to have a boyfriend because
   a. I will be able to share fun things with someone who will accept me for myself.
   b. It will be cool to have one because all of my friends do, and I feel left out.
   c. I really need someone to go to the school dance with me in a few weeks.

2. If you have a crush on a guy, what do you think is so great about him?
   a. He is really funny and smart, and he's nice to me.
   b. All of my friends think he is really hot.
   c. He is the most popular guy in school, and everyone knows him.

3. What do you think of the saying "Happily ever after"?
   a. I think it is romantic.
   b. Happily ever after what?
   c. It's true only if he is rich and will buy me tons of stuff.

4. Do your friends pressure you to like certain guys?
   a. No way. I have a lot of different friends, and they respect who I like.
   b. Yeah, sometimes they say I can't hang out with them if they are going on a group date and I don't have a boyfriend. Or I feel left out when I call my friends and they are out with their boyfriends.
   c. Yeah, because they say I will be more popular if I like or go out with certain guys.

5. Have you ever had a boyfriend before?
   a. Yes
   b. No
   c. Not really, but I told everyone I did over the summer so I would fit in.

6. What is the dating scene at your school?
   a. I don't really pay attention to anyone other than my friends, and some of us are single, and some have boyfriends.
   b. Everyone has a boyfriend, or if they don't, they are about to hook up with someone.
   c. All of the popular girls have boyfriends.

From *Girls in Real-Life Situations: Group Counseling Activities for Enhancing Social and Emotional Development—Grades 6–12*
© 2007 by J. V. Taylor and S. Trice-Black. Champaign, IL: Research Press. (800–519–2707, www.researchpress.com)

To Date or Not to Date (continued)

Now, total up your responses. (Simply count the number of responses that match up with each lettered comment.)

A's _____ B's _____ C's _____

If you scored mostly A's:

It seems that you are ready to have a boyfriend. You have a good head on your shoulders and know what you really want.

If you scored mostly B's:

It seems that the pressure to have a boyfriend is influencing your decision. If you are feeling left out of social situations, try to talk to your friends and schedule some time alone with them. Reevaluate what you are seeking in a relationship so you don't make any hasty decisions.

If you scored mostly C's:

It seems that you are really trying to fit in with a particular crowd at school. It is time for you to reevaluate your friendships and values. You need to do some serious soul-searching before you are ready to date!

Under Pressure

RATIONALE

In middle school and high school, girls normally find it difficult to cope with the sexual aspect of relationships. When they enter middle school, most girls are in the exploration stage of their sexuality and sexual identity. When they enter high school, they are bombarded with sexual pressure that is both external and internal. In both instances, girls are faced with a society filled with sexual images, pressures, and innuendos. As a result, they tend to believe that they need to be sexually active to fit in. In this activity, girls will gain insight into their beliefs in this area.

MATERIALS

Three large pieces of paper or posterboard with YES written on one, NO on another, and MAYBE SO on the last

A marker

PROCEDURE

1. Begin the group with a discussion about sexual pressure. Read the following statement: "Peer pressure is often pressure put on oneself to fit into a particular group." Ask the girls if they agree with that statement and then discuss.

2. Tell the girls that you are going to read them a list of statements and ask them, after you read each statement, to raise their hands if they agree, disagree, or don't know. Record on each poster the number of girls who respond to each statement in that way.

   a. Most girls are sexually active.

   b. You should never talk to your parents about boyfriends or sex.

   c. If your boyfriend wants to go all the way and you have been dating for more than a month, he deserves it.

   d. If you choose not to be sexually active, it means you are a prude.

e. If you go out with a lot of different guys, it means you are a slut.

f. Oral sex is not really sex.

g. It is OK to have oral sex because you can't get pregnant.

h. TV shows, movies, and magazines often show girls having multiple sex partners. They rarely get pregnant or acquire sexually transmitted diseases (STDs), so it must be OK.

i. Your parents would ground you forever if they knew you had a boyfriend, so it is OK to keep it from them and lie about where you are.

j. Most girls are not virgins by the time they graduate from high school.

k. You can't get pregnant if you have sexual intercourse while you're having your period.

l. Making out is not really cheating.

m. If you say no to a guy, he might not want to go out with you or date you anymore.

If you have other statements that may pertain to your particular group, feel free to add them.

3. Discuss the girls' responses and dispel any myths. When you have finished, encourage the girls to talk to their parents, or a trusted adult, about issues regarding sex and sexuality.

4. Discuss the sexual images and sexual messages that the media send to girls every day.

CLOSING QUESTIONS

❀ Do you feel that girls are under more pressure, sexually, than guys? Why or why not?

❀ What are the differences in the way girls and guys are labeled when it comes to sex and sexuality?

❀ How will you use what you have learned today in the future?

He Loves Me, He Loves Me Not

RATIONALE

Unfortunately, many teens have been physically, emotionally, or sexually abused by their partners. It is not uncommon for young women to think of an abusive relationship solely as physical abuse. In this lesson, the girls will learn about the different types of dating violence, how to recognize an unhealthy relationship, and how to get help.

MATERIALS

A copy of the Dating Violence Scenarios for each girl

PROCEDURE

1. Start off with a discussion about teen abuse. Ask the girls if they want to share any experiences they have had with abusive relationships. You can also ask them if they have witnessed adults in an abusive relationship.

2. Tell the girls that a lot of people have been involved in abusive relationships.

3. Explain to the girls that dating violence is not just physical abuse; it can also be emotional or sexual—or all three. Have the girls discuss the differences between the three.

4. Hand out a copy of the Dating Violence Scenarios to each girl.

5. Read each scenario aloud to the girls and ask the following questions:

    ❀ What type of abuse is occurring?

    ❀ What would you do if the female victim was you or your friend?

6. End the lesson with a discussion of where to go for help. Have each girl name different adults she feels she can go to, if necessary, and provide phone numbers to local women's shelters.

7. Encourage the girls to talk to their parents about dating abuse and what to do if they get into a situation where they need help. This is often an uncomfortable topic to discuss with parents, but it is also potentially lifesaving.

CLOSING QUESTIONS

❀ What have you learned today about dating violence?

❀ What steps can you take to ensure that you won't get caught up in an unhealthy relationship?

❀ How will you use what you have learned today in the future?

Dating Violence Scenarios

Scenario 1

Alicia and Kevin are in the 10th grade and have been going out since middle school. Recently, Alicia started noticing Kevin's getting really jealous when Alicia talks to other guys. First, Kevin would question her, saying, "Is that my competition or something?" or "What are you talking to him for? He was looking you up and down." Now, Kevin won't let Alicia even talk to another guy. He threatens to hurt the guys who talk to her and is always waiting for Alicia after school. He goes through the cell numbers in her phone and checks her e-mail to make sure she is not talking to any boys. Last week, he started writing her letters that said she could not talk to anyone else, even her girlfriends, if she wanted to stay with him, and that if she loved him, all she would want to do was think about him. Kevin even started telling Alicia what she could and could not wear and told her not to put on makeup or paint her fingernails. Alicia has dumped all of her friends and speaks only to Kevin. Her grades have suffered, and she seems really sad during the day.

Scenario 2

Carrie and Steven are in the 8th grade and have been going out for two months. They are the perfect couple and have tons of friends. They are very affectionate toward one another, and everyone says, "Awwwwww," when they see them in the hall together. Carrie's parents are never home after school, and Carrie and Steven always go over to her house and hang out. Recently, Steven has been pressuring Carrie to have sex with him, but Carrie doesn't want to. Steven told her, "If you really love me, you will," and that he would break up with her if she didn't, so she gave in. Carrie felt really disgusting afterward and cried for a week. She didn't tell any of her friends what she had done. Now, Steven wants to have sex every day, and Carrie has started coming up with excuses like "My mom is home from work this week" or "I have to stay after to get extra help in math." Steven got angry and told all of his friends, and they now call Carrie names like "easy" and "slut." He denied telling anyone about the sex and said that he loved her—but if she didn't want to keep having sex with him, their relationship was over.

Scenario 3

Shandy and Tommy are in the 11th grade and have been going out for six months. They both like to hang out with their friends and go

From *Girls in Real-Life Situations: Group Counseling Activities for Enhancing Social and Emotional Development—Grades 6–12* © 2007 by J. V. Taylor and S. Trice-Black. Champaign, IL: Research Press. (800–519–2707, www.researchpress.com)

to parties. Tommy sometimes drinks at the parties and gets really angry, sometimes for no reason. At the last party they were at, Tommy drove and promised not to drink. He did not keep his promise and was not in any condition to drive home. Shandy didn't have a license, so she said she would call her mom to pick her up. Tommy flipped out and said he would get in trouble and that she couldn't do that. He took her cell and threw it into the road and demanded that she get in the car with him. Shandy started crying. Tommy thought that somebody would hear her, so he grabbed her arm and told her to shut up. She was crying harder, and he opened the door and pushed her into the car. Her legs were hanging out and she was trying to push the door open, so he slammed it, hard, on her legs. Shandy was hysterical and bleeding, and Tommy kept slamming the door until she put her legs inside. He screamed at her the whole way home and warned her that if she told anybody, he would deny it and break up with her. Shandy loves him and knows he would never do this if he were sober. She wore long pants until the bruises went away and didn't tell anybody.

Breaking Up Is Hard to Do

RATIONALE

Breaking up is almost inevitable with teen relationships. Sometimes they just fizzle out, and sometimes they are devastating. Moving on is a necessity. In this activity, the girls will design a G.I.R.L.S. Guide to Surviving a Breakup. They will discuss and record essential tools needed, how to stay motivated, and how actually to "break up" with someone else.

MATERIALS

A copy of I Will Survive! The G.I.R.L.S. Guide to Surviving a Breakup for each girl

Colored markers, glitter pens, colored pencils, erasers, other art supplies

PROCEDURE

1. Begin the group by asking the girls how many of them have had someone break up with them. Discuss.

2. Ask the girls how many of them have broken up with someone else and discuss. Tell the girls that today they will be designing a breaking-up survival guide.

3. Go over the guide with them and allow them to list freely any options they come up with. Remind them that this tool is designed to help them get through the breakup in a positive way because stewing, seeking revenge, plotting, and refusing to let go will only hurt them. If negativity creeps in, use it as an opportunity for discussion, but allow the girls to create their own guide.

4. When they have finished, praise the healthy responses they listed and remind them that life always goes on.

CLOSING QUESTIONS

❀ What is the most difficult part of a relationship that ends in a breakup?

❀ What is healthy about moving forward?

❀ How will you use what you have learned today in the future?

I Will Survive! The G.I.R.L.S. Guide to Surviving a Breakup

Directions: Create a guide to surviving a breakup. Brainstorm with others some responses to the following headlines. You will see one example below each headline; the rest is up to you. Be creative and have fun!

Essential tools needed during a breakup:

Tissues

Essential motivating music to play:

"I Will Survive," by Gloria Gaynor or Cake

Signs that your relationship is headed south:

He won't return any of your phone calls, instant messages, or e-mails.

How to tell him "It's over!"

Make sure that *you* do the talking; don't send a friend to tell him that you two are finished.

How to react if he tells you "It's over!"

Don't fall to the floor, hysterical, in front of him.

From *Girls in Real-Life Situations: Group Counseling Activities for Enhancing Social and Emotional Development—Grades 6–12*
© 2007 by J. V. Taylor and S. Trice-Black. Champaign, IL: Research Press. (800–519–2707, www.researchpress.com)

I Will Survive! (continued)

What to do when you see him:
    Smile and act as though you are not fazed.

How to avoid seeing him
    Don't spy on him where he always hangs out.

How to still hang out with mutual friends
    Remember the things you had in common individually—not as a "couple."

What to do with all of those "reminders" of him:
    Go through your e-mails and delete every message from him.

What to do when you see him with another girl:
    Never physically or verbally attack him or her.

Finally, how to move on:
    Don't ever compare your new boyfriend to your old one, especially not in front of him!

Talk about It

Relationships

1. What would you do if you had feelings for a good guy friend?
2. Do you know anyone who has been or is in an abusive relationship?
3. Do you think that verbal abuse is just as bad as physical abuse in a relationship?
4. Talk about a time when a friend of yours has dropped you or ignored you when she is dating someone.
5. Have you ever let your friendships slide when you are in a new relationship?
6. Talk about being in love.
7. Have you ever had feelings for someone you have never met, such as someone you've met online?
8. Do you talk to your parents about dating, relationships, or sex (or all three)?
9. When do you think teens should be allowed to date? Are you allowed to date?
10. Do you know anyone who has gotten pregnant as a teenager?
11. What do you do when you really like somebody, but that person doesn't have the same feelings for you?
12. Is it ever OK to date someone a good friend of yours has dated?
13. How do you break up with someone?
14. Do you act differently around guys?
15. Talk about a time you felt that a guy was just using you or a friend.
16. Talk about a time you were jealous of a friend's relationship.
17. What is the difference between messing around and hooking up? Is it OK to hook up with someone you are not in a relationship with?
18. What role do drugs and alcohol play in hooking up?
19. Who could you go to if you found yourself in an unsafe situation with a guy?
20. Describe the perfect date and what makes it so perfect!

From *Girls in Real-Life Situations: Group Counseling Activities for Enhancing Social and Emotional Development—Grades 6–12*
© 2007 by J. V. Taylor and S. Trice-Black. Champaign, IL: Research Press. (800–519–2707, www.researchpress.com)

Think about It

Relationships

Directions: Ask yourself the following questions.

❀ What are the qualities that are important for a lasting relationship?

❀ What makes a relationship healthy?

❀ What makes a relationship unhealthy?

Now, think of five couples you know who have been happily married for a long time. List them here:

Couple #1: _____

Couple #2: _____

Couple #3: _____

Couple #4: _____

Couple #5: _____

Now list the qualities that are important to you, now or down the road, in choosing a partner. Think about your values, hobbies, interests, and goals in life. When the time comes, take a look at this list and make sure that your needs are going to be met.

Optional Journaling Questions

❀ What have your past relationships been like?

❀ How do you envision the "perfect" relationship?

From *Girls in Real-Life Situations: Group Counseling Activities for Enhancing Social and Emotional Development—Grades 6–12*
© 2007 by J. V. Taylor and S. Trice-Black. Champaign, IL: Research Press. (800–519–2707, www.researchpress.com)

Check It Out

Relationships

Here are some great books for teens. Check them out!

❀ *May I Kiss You? A Candid Look at Dating, Communication, Respect, and Sexual Assault Awareness,* by Michael Domitrz (Wailuku, HI: Awareness Publications, 2003).

❀ *A Smart Girl's Guide to Boys: Surviving Crushes, Staying True to Yourself and Other Stuff,* by Nancy Holyoke and Bonnie Timmons (Middleton, WI: Pleasant Company Publications, 2001).

❀ *Who Am I without Him? Short Stories about Girls and the Boys in Their Lives,* by Sharon G. Flake (New York: Jump at the Sun, 2007).

❀ *The Girls' Guide to Guys: Straight Talk for Teens on Flirting, Dating, Breaking Up, Making Up and Finding True Love,* by Julie Taylor (New York: Three Rivers Press, 2000).

❀ *Burned,* by Ellen Hopkins (New York: Simon and Schuster, 2006).

From *Girls in Real-Life Situations: Group Counseling Activities for Enhancing Social and Emotional Development—Grades 6–12*
© 2007 by J. V. Taylor and S. Trice-Black. Champaign, IL: Research Press. (800–519–2707, www.researchpress.com)

Self-Esteem

Connect!

Self-Esteem

Time

10 minutes

Objective

To encourage girls to make positive statements about themselves as well as others

Materials

One large bag of colored candy, such as M&M's

Activity

Have the girls sit or stand in a circle. Pass around the bag of candy, and have each girl look inside the bag and pick out one piece. After each girl selects a piece of candy, have her answer a few questions based on the color of candy she chose.

Red: Name something you like about your personality.

Green: Name something, such as a sport or hobby, that you enjoy.

Blue: Name something positive about the way you look.

Yellow: Name something unique about the girl on your right.

Brown: Name something you like about the girl on your left.

Orange: Name something positive about one girl in the group.

After this activity, give each girl some candy to enjoy while discussing the process questions.

Process Questions

❀ How did it feel to say something positive about yourself?

❀ How did it feel to say something positive about others?

❀ How did it feel to hear someone say something positive about you?

❀ Do you think it is easy for us to say positive things about ourselves and others?

❀ What do you think would help us say positive things about ourselves and others more often?

Personal Permission Slip

RATIONALE

Due to struggles with self-esteem, girls often have unrealistic expectations of themselves and are therefore afraid to try new things. The fear of failure and the demand for perfection make it difficult for girls to accept themselves. This activity encourages girls to give themselves permission to try new things and to rid themselves of unrealistic expectations.

MATERIALS

A copy of the Free to Be ME! pledge for each girl

Pencils or pens

Colored markers

A large sheet of posterboard, labeled at the top "I'm Free!"

Scissors

Glue

PROCEDURE

1. Explain to the girls that today they will be able to give themselves permission to do something they have always needed or wanted to do. This may mean that they are giving themselves permission to wipe out a certain unhealthy feeling, such as guilt or shame, and redirect that feeling to a healthy feeling. The permission may be to try something they have always wanted to do. The permission may be to talk to someone about a problem. The permission may be not to have unrealistic expectations of themselves.

2. Hand out the Free to Be ME! pledge to each girl.

3. After each girl completes her personal permission slip, instruct all the girls to cut around their pledges and glue them to the "I'm Free" poster.

4. Allow the girls to decorate the "I'm Free" poster with drawings and phrases that inspire them to fulfill the action written on their personal permission slips.

5. After they have finished decorating the poster, discuss high expectations and the "I'm Free" collage. Encourage the girls to allow themselves to do what makes them feel great about themselves every day, and tell them that they should not need special permission to feel good!

CLOSING QUESTIONS

❀ Why do you think it is sometimes difficult for girls to ease up and give themselves a break or to try something new?

❀ What do you think will help you to take the action you wrote on your personal permission slip?

❀ How will you use what you have learned today in the future?

Free to Be ME!

Today, I give myself permission to:

_____

_____

_____

_____

_____

I will feel no guilt or shame and will feel awesome about my decision ALL DAY!

Signature _____ Date _____

From *Girls in Real-Life Situations: Group Counseling Activities for Enhancing Social and Emotional Development—Grades 6–12*
© 2007 by J. V. Taylor and S. Trice-Black. Champaign, IL: Research Press. (800–519–2707, www.researchpress.com)

Shoulda, Woulda, Coulda

RATIONALE

Girls often pressure themselves with unrealistic expectations of themselves. "Should" statements, such as "I should get better grades," "I should be a better athlete," and "I should be prettier," set up girls for disappointment in themselves, which lowers their self-esteem. This activity focuses on helping girls to reframe and restate "should" statements into alternative, realistic statements.

MATERIALS

Small trash can

A copy of the Shoulda, Woulda, Coulda handout and an envelope for each girl

Pencils or pens

PROCEDURE

1. Explain to the girls that they will be exploring irrational, unrealistic expectations that girls often have about themselves.

2. Give each girl the "I should" page of the Shoulda, Woulda, Coulda handout and have each girl list 10 things she thinks she *should* do.

3. After the girls have completed their lists, ask them to share some of their "I should" statements. Encourage the girls to talk about the unrealistic expectations of "I should" statements.

4. Give each girl the "I wish" page of the Shoulda, Woulda, Coulda handout. Tell the girls to help one another restate their "I should" statements so that they become positive statements, such as changing "I should get better grades" to "I wish I could get better grades, but I study hard and am doing the best I can!"

5. After everyone has completed 10 new, positive statements, have the girls rip up their "I should" statements and toss them in the trash can.

6. Have the girls discuss their reactions to throwing away their "I should" statements.

CLOSING QUESTIONS

❊ Why do you think girls often set unrealistic goals and expectations for themselves?

❊ How do you think girls feel when they cannot meet these unrealistic goals?

❊ How will you use what you have learned today in the future?

Shoulda, Woulda, Coulda

1. I should _____

_____

2. I should _____

_____

3. I should _____

_____

4. I should _____

_____

5. I should _____

_____

6. I should _____

_____

7. I should _____

_____

8. I should _____

_____

9. I should _____

_____

10. I should _____

_____

From *Girls in Real-Life Situations: Group Counseling Activities for Enhancing Social and Emotional Development—Grades 6–12*
© 2007 by J. V. Taylor and S. Trice-Black. Champaign, IL: Research Press. (800–519–2707, www.researchpress.com)

Shoulda, Woulda, Coulda (continued)

1. I wish _____

   _____

2. I wish _____

   _____

3. I wish _____

   _____

4. I wish _____

   _____

5. I wish _____

   _____

6. I wish _____

   _____

7. I wish _____

   _____

8. I wish _____

   _____

9. I wish _____

   _____

10. I wish _____

    _____

Nobody's Perfect

RATIONALE

Because so many girls have unrealistic expectations, it helps if they have real-life examples of females who, despite their lives having not turned out the way they expected, still have been successful. It helps for girls to have role models with whom they can identify. In discussing these real-life situations, it is the hope that girls will be willing to take risks in search of higher rewards and achievements.

MATERIALS

Slips of paper

Pencils or pens

Shoe box

PROCEDURE

1. Begin the group by discussing the difficulties and pressures of trying to be perfect. Invite the girls to discuss disappointments and struggles they have faced in their lives.

2. Offer the girls examples of females who have been successful despite setbacks: Bethany Hamilton, the young woman who survived a shark attack as a surfer, continued to surf with only one arm, and even went on to a modeling career. Oprah Winfrey, one of the wealthiest and most successful women in the world, suffered many setbacks early in her career. She was constantly criticized for her weight problems and was even fired from one television station. Imagine how easy it would have been for Bethany or Oprah to give up during her difficulties. Instead, each woman persisted, achieved her goals, and eventually became successful.

3. In a roundtable format, have each girl name something she has accomplished despite difficulties.

4. After the discussion, give each girl a slip of paper and a pencil or pen.

5. Instruct each girl to write down something she would like to achieve before the group ends—a goal she would like to set for herself. Her goal might be better grades in a certain subject, getting along better with a friend, or perhaps developing a healthy habit. Each girl's goal should be personal and does not need to be shared with others.

6. After writing down the goal, each girl should place the slip of paper in the box.

7. Write on the shoe box, DON'T-GIVE-UP BOX. The girls will decorate and then seal the box to assure privacy.

8. After the activity is completed, have the girls discuss how they feel about setting a goal and the ways they intend to make sure they don't quit striving to reach it.

9. Let the girls know that you will open the box to see whether they have achieved their goals. (Indicate a time that is convenient for you.)

CLOSING QUESTIONS

❀ What does it feel like to set goals for yourself?

❀ How will you use what you have learned today in the future?

My Brag Bag

RATIONALE

Achieving a positive self-concept and healthy self-esteem are a struggle for many girls. It is often difficult for girls to think about the positive aspects of their lives. Often they focus on difficulties, rather than realizing their own personal success and potential. This activity is aimed at helping girls focus on personal achievements and strengths in order to help promote self-esteem.

MATERIALS

Small paper bags

A copy of the My Bragging Rights handout for each girl

Scissors

Colored markers

Pencils or pens

PROCEDURE

1. Begin the discussion with a mention of the importance of a positive self-concept. Explain to the girls that *self-concept* refers to the way we view ourselves.

2. Invite the girls to talk about the reasons it is important to have a positive self-concept. Discuss those things that may lower our self-esteem and make it harder for us to believe in ourselves.

3. Tell the girls that in order to help develop a positive self-concept and to raise self-esteem, people must be able to identify and believe in positive aspects of their lives.

4. Ask the girls what they think about people who brag.

5. Tell the girls that today they will brag about themselves and will view bragging as a healthy way to improve their self-concept.

6. Give each girl a copy of the My Brag Blog handout and a paper bag. Place the markers and scissors in an accessible location.

7. Allow the girls a few minutes to complete the My Brag Blog handout and then have them cut out their brags.

8. Allow time for them to decorate their brown brag bags. Explain that the bags are for the girls to keep as reminders of the positive aspects of who they are and who they are continuing to become.

9. After the decorating is completed, have the girls share at least one brag from their bags with the rest of the group.

CLOSING QUESTIONS

❀ Which brag was the most difficult to complete?

❀ Why do you think girls have a hard time concentrating on the positive aspects of their lives?

❀ How will you use what you have learned today in the future?

My Bragging Rights

Directions: Write down everything you think is great about you!

From *Girls in Real-Life Situations: Group Counseling Activities for Enhancing Social and Emotional Development—Grades 6–12*
© 2007 by J. V. Taylor and S. Trice-Black. Champaign, IL: Research Press. (800–519–2707, www.researchpress.com)

Talk about It

Self-Esteem

1. Define the word *self-esteem.*
2. What are some things that help your self-esteem, and what are some things that hurt your self-esteem?
3. Talk about someone who has put you down or made you feel bad about yourself. What was your response, and how did the experience affect you?
4. What activities make you feel great about yourself?
5. How do you reward yourself when you do something spectacular?
6. Do you find it hard to brag to your friends about the good qualities you possess?
7. What does it mean to stay true to yourself and your values?
8. Talk about some of your values and where you got them.
9. How do you think your self-esteem determines your mood and the day you are going to have?
10. What is your biggest accomplishment?
11. How have you helped a friend's self-esteem?
12. How have you hurt a friend's self-esteem?
13. Do you know someone who always has to one-up another person? Talk about how that feels.
14. Why do you think some people have high self-esteem and others have low self-esteem?
15. Talk about a time you compared yourself to someone else and felt bad about it afterward.
16. Do you ever feel like your brain just won't stop putting you down?
17. Is it ever good to be critical of yourself?
18. What are some of the terms you think your friends would use to describe you? Do you believe them?
19. What is your favorite thing about yourself?
20. What are some things you are willing to try to enhance the way you feel about yourself?

From *Girls in Real-Life Situations: Group Counseling Activities for Enhancing Social and Emotional Development—Grades 6–12*
© 2007 by J. V. Taylor and S. Trice-Black. Champaign, IL: Research Press. (800–519–2707, www.researchpress.com)

Think about It

Self-Esteem

Directions: Make a list of 25 things you like to do that make you feel awesome about yourself. The next time you are feeling bored, down, lonely, or just plain silly, pick something from the list and start feeling better!

1. _____
2. _____
3. _____
4. _____
5. _____
6. _____
7. _____
8. _____
9. _____
10. _____
11. _____
12. _____
13. _____

14. _____
15. _____
16. _____
17. _____
18. _____
19. _____
20. _____
21. _____
22. _____
23. _____
24. _____
25. _____

Optional Journaling Questions

❀ What are some of the things you think are great about yourself, but refuse to flaunt?

❀ What makes it hard to flaunt those qualities?

From *Girls in Real-Life Situations: Group Counseling Activities for Enhancing Social and Emotional Development—Grades 6–12*
© 2007 by J. V. Taylor and S. Trice-Black. Champaign, IL: Research Press. (800–519–2707, www.researchpress.com)

Check It Out

Self-Esteem

Here are some great books for teens. Check them out!

❀ *Real Girl, Real World: A Guide to Finding Your True Self,* by Heather M. Gray and Samantha Phillips (Emoryville, CA: Seal Press, 2005).

❀ *Bodypride: An Action Plan for Teens Seeking Self-Esteem and Building Better Bodies,* by Cynthia Stamper Graff, Janet Eastman, and Mark C. Smith (Spokane, WA: Griffin Publishing, 1997).

❀ *Stick Up for Yourself: Every Kid's Guide to Personal Power and Positive Self-Esteem,* by Gershen Kaufman, Lev Raphael, and Pamela Espeland (Minneapolis: Free Spirit Publishing, 1999).

❀ *Teen Esteem: A Self-Direction Manual for Young Adults,* by Pat Palmer and Melissa Alberti Froehner (Atascadero, CA: Little Imp Books, 2000).

❀ *Be True to Yourself: A Daily Guide for Teenage Girls,* by Amanda Ford (Berkeley, CA: Conari Press, 2000).

From *Girls in Real-Life Situations: Group Counseling Activities for Enhancing Social and Emotional Development—Grades 6–12*
© 2007 by J. V. Taylor and S. Trice-Black. Champaign, IL: Research Press. (800–519–2707, www.researchpress.com)

Stress

Connect!

Stress

Time
10 minutes

Objective
For the girls to identify sources of stress and help each other deal with their stressors.

Materials
Deck of playing cards

A box (or another container)

Paper

Pencils or pens

Preparation
Select a pair of cards of the same denomination for each pair of girls (two queens, two tens, etc.) Put the cards in the box.

Activity
Have the girls draw cards from the box. Instruct the girls to find the other person in the group who has the same card. After finding their card partner, have the girls work together in pairs and make a list of the top five stressors in their lives. After completion, ask the partners to share their lists with the group.

Process Questions
❀ What similar stressors did the pairs share?

❀ What are some ideas that could help you avoid these stressors?

❀ What are some things you can do to help you feel better when you are faced with these stressors?

Deal with It!

RATIONALE

Stress is an inevitable part of life. How we deal with stress determines the number of physical and mental symptoms we incur because of it. Girls often believe they have no control over the stress in their lives and frequently have a difficult time accepting responsibility for what they bring on themselves. This activity teaches the girls about different situations that bring on stress. By discussing stressors, the girls should be able to help one another come up with coping mechanisms for dealing with stress.

MATERIALS

Index cards

Pencils or pens

PROCEDURE

1. Begin the discussion by asking the girls what stresses them out.
2. Ask the girls how they deal with the stress that they are aware of.
3. When the girls are done speaking, explain to them the AAA's of stress management:

   You can *avoid* the stress that you bring on yourself, *accept* the stress that you have no control over, and *adjust* the stress you have control over by changing the way you think about it.

Avoid

Ask the girls to talk about a problem they are responsible for causing. Here are some examples:

❀ They hang around friends who get them into trouble.
❀ They take part in too many after-school activities, and thus have little free time.
❀ They don't do their homework on time, which forces them to study for tests at the last minute.

4. Have each girl take an index card and instruct her to do the following: On one side of the card, she is to write down two stressors she is responsible for causing. On the other side, she is to write down two ways she can help manage the two stressors.

Accept

Ask the girls to talk about some of the factors that cause stress that they find they cannot control. Some examples:
Their parents are going through a divorce.

❀ They recently moved to a new town and don't have many friends.

❀ They cannot hang out with friends a lot on the weekends because they have to go out of town with their parents.

5. This time, have each girl write down on one side of an index card two stressors she cannot control. On the other side, have her write down two ways she can think differently so she will be able to accept both situations.

Adjust

Ask the girls to talk about some of the stress in their lives that they feel they can change. Examples:

❀ If they are habitually turning in homework late, they can make a plan to start it early.

❀ If they don't have enough time to get ready for school in the morning, they can go to bed earlier so they can wake up earlier.

❀ If they repeatedly get into fights with their parents or friends, they can try to see others' points of view.

6. Have each girl label the appropriate index card with AVOID, ADJUST, or ACCEPT at the top.

7. On a new index card, have each girl write down two recent stressors that she feels she can avoid, adjust to, and accept on one side of an index card.

8. Have each girl think of one action plan per stressor on the other side.

9. In a roundtable format, discuss each girl's stressors and some alternative coping mechanisms to the ones she jotted on the index card.

CLOSING QUESTIONS

❀ What have you learned about your stress management today?

❀ What are you willing to do in order to reduce the amount of stress in your daily life?

❀ How will you use what you have learned today in the future?

Facing Fear

RATIONALE

Fear is the underlying cause of anxiety. Girls experience multiple anxieties and fear-provoking changes that consistently rattle them. Their fears may lead to avoidance and might significantly and adversely affect their lives if not confronted. This activity allows the girls to identify the fears they have and to figure out the amount of interference these fears are causing in their lives. It calls on each of them to choose her biggest fear and work on steps to combat it.

MATERIALS

A copy of the Facing My Fear handout for each girl

Pens or pencils

Colored markers

PROCEDURE

1. Begin the group by asking the girls, "What are you afraid of that interferes with your life?" Some common fears they will mention are speaking in front of groups, contracting a deadly disease, being around animals, talking to people they don't know, going to the cafeteria at lunch, speaking up in class, walking past groups of people, the dark, blood, eating in front of people, being alone for long periods of time, and having bad things happen to family members or close friends.

2. After the girls have called out some of their fears, discuss the difference between rational and irrational fear. (Keep in mind that, although some of their fears may seem inconceivable, irrational fears may be very real to them.)

3. Hand out a copy of Facing My Fear to each girl.

4. Instruct the girls to write their biggest fear in the center of the flower on the handout, and also list—on the petals—the steps they are willing to take to combat that fear.

5. When they are finished, invite the girls to share their fear with the group and tell the other girls the steps they plan on taking to combat it.

CLOSING QUESTIONS

❁ Are your fears mostly rational or irrational?

❁ What steps are you willing to take immediately to combat your fear?

❁ How will you use what you have learned today in the future?

Facing My Fear

From *Girls in Real-Life Situations: Group Counseling Activities for Enhancing Social and Emotional Development—Grades 6–12*
© 2007 by J. V. Taylor and S. Trice-Black. Champaign, IL: Research Press. (800–519–2707, www.researchpress.com)

Chill Out!

RATIONALE

Learning to relax can help relieve the physical symptoms of stress and help us think more clearly. Sometimes we react to stressors without taking a moment to breathe and think about the consequences of our actions. This activity shows the girls different ways to relax when facing stress.

MATERIALS

CD player and a CD of soft, mellow music

PROCEDURE

1. Begin by asking the girls how they react to stress.
2. When each girl has had a chance to speak, ask for examples of her reacting to stress in a negative way and the consequences of her quick reaction.
3. Tell the girls that today they are going to learn how to slow down their thought process when unpredictable stress occurs.
4. Decide whether you want the girls to take part in this activity while sitting on the floor or in their chairs or standing up. Read to them the following steps:
   a. Close your eyes and take a few deep breaths. Breathe in through your nose and out your mouth.
   b. Try to think of a place you like; it could be your bedroom, the beach, the woods, or some other comfortable place that you enjoy being.
   c. When you breathe in, try to fill your belly with air while counting slowly to five.
   d. When you get to five, slowly breathe out, again counting to five.
5. Have the girls continue this breathing exercise for about two minutes.

6. Next, instruct the girls to tighten every muscle in their body. Ask them to hold the tension as hard as they can for about 15 seconds and then release it with a deep "belly breath." Have the girls repeat this process a few times (until they are bored). You can also have them tense one body part at a time. For example, they can tense their left leg, then their right leg, and so on.

7. Play the mellow music and have the girls practice their relaxation techniques on their own for the remainder of the session. If they want, they can practice in different locations (standing, sitting, lying down, etc.).

CLOSING QUESTIONS

❀ When could you use these techniques to reduce your stress without anybody knowing?

❀ How will you use what you have learned today in the future?

Stress Survival Kit

RATIONALE

It is often difficult for girls to identify life stressors and even more difficult for them to deal with those stressors. Discussing common problems and developing techniques to deal with stressors can help prevent stress from developing into anxiety and depression. This activity focuses on helping girls identify and deal with their personal stressors.

MATERIALS

A large manila envelope for each girl

Index cards

Pencils or pens

Colored markers

First-aid kit

PROCEDURE

1. Show a first-aid kit to the girls. Ask them why a first-aid kit is important to have around.

2. Pass the kit around for the girls to explore. Discuss the different items in it and their purpose.

3. Talk about how the first-aid kit helps us when we are physically injured or ill by preventing further harm.

4. Ask the girls if they can fix stress with anything in the first aid kit. When they say no, tell them that we need to be prepared with the tools to deal with stressors in our lives, just as we are prepared with the tools in a first-aid kit.

5. Give each girl a manila envelope, several index cards, markers, and a pencil or pen.

6. Have the girls write down a different stressor in their lives on each index card.

7. Have each girl turn her index cards over and list the ways she can help prevent or deal with the stressor on the other side.

8. Tell each girl to place the index cards in the manila envelope and to decorate the outside of the envelope.

9. Explain that the manila envelopes will serve as stress survival kits; they will be similar to first-aid kits, but will instead include tools to deal with the stressors in the girls' lives.

10. Have each girl share the contents of her stress survival kit with the whole group.

CLOSING QUESTIONS

❊ What were some helpful ways to prevent or deal with stressors that were shared in the group?

❊ Why do you think it helps to have a plan to deal with stressors before they happen?

❊ How will you use what you have learned today in the future?

Talk about It

Stress

1. What is the difference between a situation that you have control over and a situation that you have no control over?

2. What are some situations that cause you stress and anxiety?

3. How do you compare yourself to other girls who seem to "have it easy"? For example, have you ever been jealous of a girl who never studies and gets straight A's or who has a great home life?

4. What are some things that you worry about every day? Do you have control over your concerns?

5. How do your parents deal with stress?

6. What are you afraid of? How much does fear interfere with your life?

7. What do you avoid because of fear?

8. Do you know someone who has an anxiety disorder? How does the person act? Do you wish you could change the person's behaviors?

9. How often do you feel overloaded and overwhelmed?

10. Who or what do you think causes the most amount of stress in your life?

11. How do you relax in a situation that causes stress and anxiety?

12. What are some strategies you have tried to manage your stress?

13. Talk about steps you can take to prevent stress and anxiety in your life.

14. When was the last time that you were able to relax in a situation that would normally upset you?

15. What are some of the physical symptoms that you develop when you become stressed out and anxious?

16. Give some examples of controllable and uncontrollable situations you often face that cause stress.

17. What are some unhealthy things that people do to control stress?

18. What are some of the character traits of people you know who are really stressed out?

19. When do you recall laughing at a friend or family member because he or she was freaking out about something you did not think was a big deal?

20. What are some stress-management techniques that have worked for you when you are feeling overwhelmed?

From *Girls in Real-Life Situations: Group Counseling Activities for Enhancing Social and Emotional Development—Grades 6–12*
© 2007 by J. V. Taylor and S. Trice-Black. Champaign, IL: Research Press. (800–519–2707, www.researchpress.com)

Think about It

Stress

Directions: Everyone experiences stress, and everyone deals with stress differently. You can have healthy and unhealthy reactions to stress; the choice is yours. In the space below, describe two situations that often cause you to be stressed out and the different responses you choose to give— one unhealthy response and one healthy response for each situation.

Stressful situation 1

Unhealthy reaction: _____

Healthy reaction: _____

Stressful situation 2

Unhealthy reaction: _____

Healthy reaction: _____

Optional Journaling Questions

❀ Are your reactions to stress generally healthy or unhealthy?

❀ What are some stressful situations that you can react to differently?

From *Girls in Real-Life Situations: Group Counseling Activities for Enhancing Social and Emotional Development—Grades 6–12*
© 2007 by J. V. Taylor and S. Trice-Black. Champaign, IL: Research Press. (800–519–2707, www.researchpress.com)

Check It Out

Stress

Here are some great books for teens. Check them out!

❀ *Organizing from the Inside Out for Teenagers: The Foolproof System for Organizing Your Room, Your Time, and Your Life,* by Julie Morgenstern and Jessi Morgenstern-Colon (New York: Henry Holt, 2002).

❀ *Dealing with the Stuff That Makes Life Tough: The 10 Things That Stress Teen Girls Out and How to Cope with Them,* by Jill Zimmerman Rutledge (New York: McGraw-Hill, 2003).

❀ *Girls under Pressure,* by Jacqueline Wilson (London, England: Young Corgi, 2003).

❀ *A Taste-Berry Teen's Guide to Managing the Stress and Pressures of Life,* by Bettie Youngs and Jennifer Youngs (Deerfield Beach, FL: Health Communications Inc., 2001).

❀ *Complete Idiot's Guide to Dealing with Stress for Teens,* by Sara Jane Sluke, Vanessa Torres, and Jody P. Schaeffer (Minneapolis, MN: Tandem Library, 2001).

From *Girls in Real-Life Situations: Group Counseling Activities for Enhancing Social and Emotional Development—Grades 6–12*
© 2007 by J. V. Taylor and S. Trice-Black. Champaign, IL: Research Press. (800–519–2707, www.researchpress.com)

Reaching Out

Connect!

Reaching Out

Time

10 minutes

Objective

The girls will spend time in a situation where they must trust and depend on someone else and in a situation where they must help another person.

Materials

Blindfolds

Activity

Divide the girls into pairs. Explain that one girl from each group will be blindfolded and that the other girl must act as her eyes. The pair must go on a short walk around the room. After a few minutes, instruct the girls to trade places and let the other girl spend some time wearing the blindfold.

Process Questions

❀ How did it feel to be blindfolded and to have to depend on someone else?

❀ How did it feel to have someone else have to depend on you to walk around the room?

❀ Do you think it is hard for us to reach out to others for help? Explain why or why not.

❀ Do you think it is hard for us to help others in difficult situations? Explain why or why not.

I'm OK, You're OK!

RATIONALE

Girls often struggle with asking for help from friends, family, and other adults when they think they have failed. Their fear of asking for help comes from embarrassment and unwillingness to admit fault. This activity shows the girls that sometimes, no matter how hard we try, we fail. It will teach the girls that when they fail, they have to pull themselves together and move on.

MATERIALS

A balloon (not blown up) and permanent marker for each girl

Cup, small box, basket, or container

Money, candy, cool pencils, nail polish, or other small incentives that a girl would enjoy

PROCEDURE

1. Begin the group by asking the girls about something they tried really hard to succeed at but failed. It could be a sport, an art project—anything they attempted to do their best at but just couldn't.

2. Ask the girls if someone told them to try again, or harder, or said, "You didn't try your best." Discuss their feelings about those statements, with their knowing they *did* try their best.

3. Ask the girls to describe how they attempted to let the person know they did try or how they felt when they tried again but failed.

4. Give each girl a balloon and instruct her to write her initials or name on it but not to blow it up.

5. Take out the container and set it down across the room—at least seven feet from the group.

6. Take out the incentive you chose to use and place it by the container.

7. Tell the girls that if someone can blow up the balloon—and not tie it—let it deflate, and have it land in the container, she can have the incentive. Chances, of course, are very slim that this will happen.

8. Have the girls blow up their balloons and let them deflate a few times.

9. Reassemble the group and ask the girls how badly they wanted the incentive. Ask them if they tried to get their balloon to fall into the container. Ask if they had control over the balloon and its descent. Discuss.

10. Explain to the group that sometimes, no matter what the incentive, we simply cannot do something that we really want to do—and that is OK!

11. Discuss with the girls the various ways to talk about this fact of life with parents, teachers, friends, and anyone else who might be faulting them for their inability to do something.

CLOSING QUESTIONS

❀ Who puts the most pressure on you to keep trying at something you just cannot do?

❀ How has this activity helped you to realize that it is OK to fail sometimes?

❀ How will you use what you have learned today in the future?

Wall of Support

RATIONALE

Social support for girls can help prevent depression, substance abuse, aggression, and early sexual activity. Social support for girls can help raise their self-esteem and self-confidence and can help girls develop empathy and learn to care for others around them. It is important to help girls develop a positive support group—for example, their families, school personnel, coaches, and friends—as well as positive thoughts and feelings.

MATERIALS

> Set of building blocks (enough for each girl to have at least four)
> Colored markers
> Construction paper of different colors
> Scissors, glue

PROCEDURE

1. Begin the group by using the building blocks to build a "wall."

2. Ask the girls about the various reasons for building walls (for example, walls offer protection, provide support, and separate things).

3. Explain that your block wall symbolizes a "wall of support" that can provide protection and assistance.

4. Take the blocks down and give each girl at least four blocks she can use to help build the bottom layer.

5. Instruct each girl to place one of the blocks on the bottom, or foundation, layer. Before she puts the block in place, have each girl give the name of an adult she trusts and loves.

   As the foundation, this layer often includes family, although not necessarily parents. Sometimes, extended family members or other adults close to the family are a greater source of support for girls than their parents.

176

6. Allow the girls to begin building the second layer of the wall. This second layer of support should include other adults who provide assistance and help—perhaps coaches, teachers, or administrators. Each girl should say aloud the name of somebody in this category.

7. The wall's third layer of support should include friends. Each girl should place a block on this layer after providing the name of a friend she trusts.

8. The fourth layer of support should include things that help promote positive thoughts, such as sports, art, movies, games, being outside, and other items or activities that provide relief from stress.

9. After they have finished building the wall of blocks, give the girls construction paper, scissors, glue, and markers.

10. Have the girls create their own walls of support by cutting out different-colored "blocks" of construction paper to serve as the four layers of their walls. The four different layers should include the following:

    The first, or foundation, layer: Family or other close adults who provide love and trust

    The second layer: Other adults who provide assistance and support

    The third layer: Friends who provide trust

    The fourth layer: Items and activities that provide relief from stress and promote positive thoughts

11. After everyone has finished, have each girl share her wall of support with the entire group.

CLOSING QUESTIONS

❀ When is it most important for you to remember your wall of support?

❀ What are some reasons that girls sometimes feel that they have no one to depend on?

❀ How will you use what you have learned today in the future?

Family Feuds

RATIONALE

Families can be a source both of great support and of much frustration, sadness, and anger. The push and pull that occur in families can be rewarding yet difficult. Family history, family culture, extended family relationships, family traditions, and family stories pull family members together as one unit. Problems such as family secrets, violence, hurtful words, and lies are examples of things that push family members apart. This activity helps girls explore their families and note the things that provide the push and pull that make their families unique.

MATERIALS

Two magnets for each girl

PROCEDURE

1. Show the girls a set of magnets and explain how the magnets can attract one another and fit together. Demonstrate how one magnet can actually attract and pull the other closer.

2. Show the group how the magnets can also push each other away when the opposite sides are used. Demonstrate one magnet's pushing another away.

3. Give each girl a set of magnets and encourage her to play with them, watching them attract and repel.

4. Ask the girls what they think the similarities are between the magnets and family relationships. Give examples of things such as family history, family culture, extended family relationships, and family stories that attract family members and pull them closer, the way the magnets attract each other.

5. Next, ask the girls to talk about ways that families push each other away—the way the magnets repel each other—with examples such as violence, family secrets, insults, and lies.

6. In a roundtable format, have each girl give an example (using her set of magnets) of a way that her family pulls itself together and a way that it pushes itself apart.

7. When all of the girls have taken turns, ask them to think about and share certain ways they can help keep their families strong, rather than pushing people's buttons and keeping their families at a distance.

CLOSING QUESTIONS

❀ Why do you think family members hurt each other?

❀ Why do you think it is hard for family members to talk to each other about problems?

❀ How will you use what you have learned today in the future?

Seven Days of PRAK Attacks

RATIONALE

PRAK (Practicing Random Acts of Kindness) is a way to reach out to others and help prevent aggression. By concentrating on the needs of others, people approach the world with caring and kindness. Adolescents need to be taught ways to reach out to others and spread kindness. This activity helps girls practice random acts of kindness at school, at home, and with their friends.

MATERIALS

A cup and a copy of the PRAK Attack handout for each girl

An envelope for each girl

Scissors

Pencils or pens

Colored markers

PROCEDURE

1. Explain what *PRAK* means and ask the girls to share their thoughts about the phrase.
2. Ask the girls to define the word *kindness* and then to give some examples of acts of kindness.
3. Ask the girls to talk about reasons it is important to spread kindness around.
4. Hand out a copy of PRAK Attack to each girl and have her complete the activity.
5. After everyone is finished, ask each girl to share her acts of kindness with the group.
6. After sharing, have the girls take scissors and cut out their PRAK attacks.
7. Collect the PRAKS and place them in a cup.
8. Give each girl an envelope and allow her to decorate it, writing PRAKS on the outside.

9. Have each girl pick out seven PRAKS and place them in her envelope.

10. Instruct the girls to take their envelopes home. Tell them to pick one PRAK from their envelope each day and perform the PRAK. Tell them it is extra-special when they perform a PRAK and don't tell anyone about it.

11. Ask the girls to observe the effects of their acts of kindness and to note how multiple acts of kindness affect others as well as themselves.

CLOSING QUESTIONS

❀ How do you think it would be if everyone in your school performed one act of kindness a day? What changes do you think you would see?

❀ What act of kindness would you like to see someone perform?

❀ How will you use what you have learned today in the future?

PRAK Attack

Directions: Write down seven PRAKS that you can do, or have done, on a daily basis (for example, holding the door open for someone, telling your parents thank you for dinner, and helping a friend with her homework).

PRAK Attack #1 _____

_____

PRAK Attack #2 _____

_____

PRAK Attack #3 _____

_____

PRAK Attack #4 _____

_____

PRAK Attack #5 _____

_____

PRAK Attack #6 _____

_____

PRAK Attack #7 _____

_____

From *Girls in Real-Life Situations: Group Counseling Activities for Enhancing Social and Emotional Development—Grades 6–12*
© 2007 by J. V. Taylor and S. Trice-Black. Champaign, IL: Research Press. (800–519–2707, www.researchpress.com)

<u>Talk about It</u>

Reaching Out

1. Do you find it difficult to ask for help?
2. What is the hardest subject for you to open up about?
3. Talk about trusting people.
4. Talk about a time someone betrayed your trust.
5. When someone betrays your trust, can you trust that person again?
6. Name some adults you trust and can go to for help or advice.
7. Talk about a friend you can count on 24/7—no matter what.
8. Is it important to you for your friends to be dependable?
9. Do you consider yourself a dependable friend?
10. Whom do you share your closest secrets with? Is it difficult or easy for you to do that?
11. Have you ever thought you could trust a friend, and then heard the friend say bad things or gossip about another friend? Discuss.
12. When a friend confides in you, do you find it hard to keep what he or she says a secret?
13. Give some examples of times when you should talk to a trusted adult about a problem that you or a friend is having.
14. Have your parents shared with you some of the struggles they had when they were your age?
15. Is it easier or harder to talk to guys about your problems than it is to talk to girls?
16. How do you approach someone you want to talk to about an important issue?
17. When are some inappropriate times to talk about something really important?
18. Talk about feeling guilty and the need for reassurance when it comes to talking about your problems.
19. Do you accept advice when it is given to you?
20. Talk about the difference between active and passive listening.

From *Girls in Real-Life Situations: Group Counseling Activities for Enhancing Social and Emotional Development—Grades 6–12*
© 2007 by J. V. Taylor and S. Trice-Black. Champaign, IL: Research Press. (800–519–2707, www.researchpress.com)

Think about It

Reaching Out

Directions: Who can you always count on to help you with your problems? In the space below, list two adults and two friends you can go to for help.

_____   _____

_____   _____

What is the most difficult part of asking for help when you are having a problem?

Sometimes you may need advice, and sometimes you may just want someone to listen to you. How can you tell people what you need from them without offending them?

Optional Journaling Questions

❀ What things really bother you about your friends when they are having a problem?
❀ When do you sometimes wish your friends would overreact when they are having a problem?

From Girls in Real-Life Situations: Group Counseling Activities for Enhancing Social and Emotional Development—Grades 6–12
© 2007 by J. V. Taylor and S. Trice-Black. Champaign, IL: Research Press. (800–519–2707, www.researchpress.com)

Here are some great books for teens. Check them out!

❋ *Girls: What's So Bad about Being Good? How to Have Fun, Survive the Preteen Years, and Remain True to Yourself,* by Harriet S. Mosatche and Liz Lawner (New York: Three Rivers Press, 2001).

❋ *Just Listen,* by Sarah Dessen (New York: Penguin Group, 2006).

❋ *The Giving Tree,* by Shel Silverstein (New York: HarperCollins, 1964).

❋ *Teens with the Courage to Give: Young People Who Triumphed over Tragedy and Volunteered to Make a Difference,* by Jackie Waldman (Berkeley, CA: Conari Press, 2000).

❋ *Chicken Soup for the Girl's Soul: Real Stories by Real Girls about Real Stuff,* by Jack Canfield, Mark Victor Hansen, Patty Hansen, and Irene Dunlap (Deerfield Beach, FL: Health Communications, Inc., 2005).

From *Girls in Real-Life Situations: Group Counseling Activities for Enhancing Social and Emotional Development—Grades 6–12*
© 2007 by J. V. Taylor and S. Trice-Black. Champaign, IL: Research Press. (800–519–2707, www.researchpress.com)

Tough Times

Connect!

Tough Times

Time

10 minutes

Objective

For the girls to share difficulties and continue to develop empathy for one another

Materials

Old lamp or lantern

Activity

Have the girls stay seated or ask them to stand in a circle. Briefly recap the story of Aladdin, who finds a magic lamp. When Aladdin rubs the lamp, a genie who can grant him three wishes appears. Explain that in this activity the group will pretend that the lamp or lantern is magical. Pass around the lamp or lantern and tell the girls that each one will get to share three wishes that could fix any areas of difficulty in her life.

Process Questions

❀ What was it like to imagine that you could be granted three wishes that could fix any problems?

❀ Were any of the wishes that you stated realistic?

❀ Is there any way you could help make those wishes come true?

Depression

RATIONALE

Depressed adolescents may have difficulty asserting themselves. They may have trouble expressing true feelings and asking for what they need or want, sometimes succumbing to peer pressure. True assertiveness stems from self-awareness—in other words, knowing what they are asking for. Self-awareness requires that we know about our own bodies, our own thoughts, our own wants, and our own needs.

MATERIALS

Paper

Pencils or pens

PROCEDURE

1. Explain to the group members that they will be talking about depression—its meaning and how to prevent and treat it.

2. Ask the girls to talk about depression:

   ❀ What does *depression* mean?

   ❀ How does depression affect girls today?

3. After a brief discussion, give each girl a piece of paper and a pencil or pen.

4. Instruct the girls to draw a large stick figure of a girl.

5. Ask the girls to write down, on the left side of the stick figure's head, any thoughts that may occur to a depressed person.

6. When they are done, have them write positive thoughts on the right side of the head of the stick figure—thoughts that can help prevent and deal with depression.

7. Next, instruct the girls to list feelings of depression on the left side of the body and positive feelings on the right side of the body.

8. Have the girls list, on the left side of the feet, unhealthy actions that may contribute to depression.

9. Have them list, on the right side of the feet, healthy actions that combat depression.

10. When the group has finished, invite each girl to share her picture with the group.

CLOSING QUESTIONS

❀ How do you think girls can help themselves feel better when they are depressed?

❀ What are some of the most common causes of depression in girls today?

❀ How will you use what you have learned today in the future?

Divorce

RATIONALE

The possibility of their parents getting a divorce is a common fear among adolescents today—and unfortunately a common reality. It is normal for children of divorced parents to feel that they are somehow responsible for, or a cause of, the divorce. Children of divorce need to hear that the divorce is not their fault and that it is normal to worry that in some way it was their fault. These adolescents often struggle with feelings of isolation, guilt, and shame. It is helpful for them to be able to share these feelings.

MATERIALS

Three large pieces of posterboard, labeled as follows: Fears about Divorce, How to Help a Friend Whose Parents Are Divorced, and The Reality of Your Parents' Being Divorced

Colored markers

PROCEDURE

1. Explain to the group that they will be discussing the effects of divorce on girls today. Invite the girls to share any thoughts or experiences related to divorce, such as their own personal experiences as a child of divorce or those of a friend or family member.

2. Talk to the girls about the common feelings of guilt, shame, and isolation that often exist in children of divorced parents.

3. Next, talk to the girls about the feelings of responsibility that many children of divorce have, as if the divorce were their fault.

4. After a brief discussion, show the girls the three pieces of posterboard.

5. Give each girl a marker and have her list her own feelings, thoughts, struggles, experiences, and questions on each of the posterboards.

6. The first board, Fears about Divorce, should include any statements, questions, phrases, or pictures that express feelings of fear

about their parents' relationships or feelings about divorce in general.

7. The second board, How to Help a Friend Whose Parents Are Divorced, should include statements, tips, drawings, and so on that girls think will help friends whose parents are divorced. The girls may want to write about things that have helped them or a friend. They may also want to include comments they wish others had made to them.

8. The third board, The Reality of Your Parents' Being Divorced, should include pictures, feelings, questions, and statements about the reality of the effects on themselves in particular and children of divorce generally.

9. When the girls are finished, display all of the posterboards and discuss them.

CLOSING QUESTIONS

❀ What did you learn today that would be helpful to you or a friend whose parents are divorced?

❀ How did this activity help you talk about and explore your feelings about divorce?

❀ How will you use what you have learned today in the future?

Understanding Loss

RATIONALE

In her book *On Death and Dying,* Elizabeth Kübler-Ross defines five stages of grief: denial, anger, bargaining, depression, and acceptance. As well as occurring with the loss of a loved one, these stages of grief are common with other types of loss: a divorce, loss of a friendship, loss of a pet, a recent move, and so on. Everybody moves through the stages at a different pace. In this activity, girls will, with regard to the loss of divorce, explore the different stages, identify where they are, and recognize different feelings associated with loss. If some of the girls have not experienced this type of loss, they can listen to the various ways they can help a friend who has.

MATERIALS

A copy of The Stages of Grief handout for each girl

Pencils or pens

PROCEDURE

1. Begin by asking the girls to share their experiences with grief and loss by asking questions such as these:

   ❀ Who or what in your life have you have lost?

   ❀ Is this loss the death of a loved one? If so, how did the person die? Who told you about the death or loss?

   ❀ What was your first feeling when you found out about the death or loss?

   ❀ How are you currently dealing with the death or loss?

   ❀ Allow girls to pass if they do not feel comfortable sharing.

2. Hand out The Stages of Grief to each girl and read each stage aloud.

3. Ask each girl to circle the word that represents the stage she believes she is in. Reinforce the notion that it is normal for everyone to move through the stages at a different pace and to move back and forth between the stages.

4. When they are finished, have each girl brainstorm different feelings associated with each stage and list them on the back of her handout. Her feelings may be real or what she imagines they would be.

5. Invite the girls to share with the group if they feel comfortable doing so.

CLOSING QUESTIONS

❁ How did you feel when talking about your loss?

❁ How can you take care of yourself while you are going through the stages of grief?

❁ How will you use what you have learned today in the future?

The Stages of Grief

Denial

Denial is when someone refuses to believe the reality of the situation (for example, the person doesn't want to believe someone has died or has a terminal illness.

Anger

Anger is a normal feeling associated with loss. People express their anger differently: They may be mad at the person who is sick or who died or left them; they may be angry at someone they think caused the illness or loss; or they may be angry at themselves—believing that they are responsible for the illness or death or loss.

Bargaining

Bargaining takes place when someone attempts to talk her way out of the illness or death. She may say, "I promise I will be better if you get well or come back" or "I will get better grades and keep my room clean if you don't die."

Depression

Depression means that someone feels sadness and hurt because of the illness or death.

Acceptance

Acceptance indicates that someone understands that a certain person is no longer with them or is going to die and has come to terms with the situation.

From *Girls in Real-Life Situations: Group Counseling Activities for Enhancing Social and Emotional Development—Grades 6–12*
© 2007 by J. V. Taylor and S. Trice-Black. Champaign, IL: Research Press. (800–519–2707, www.researchpress.com)

Self-Harm

RATIONALE

Self-harm means that someone deliberately injures herself. Young people, most commonly girls, often self-injure as a means of coping during difficult situations. Self-injurious behavior may take place daily or only when pressure arises. Anyone partaking in self-injurious behavior should be referred for professional help. It is important for professionals to focus on the feelings surrounding the self-harm instead of merely suggesting that the girls just stop (they may not be ready), pass judgment on the behavior (for example, saying, "That is so gross. I don't know why someone would do that"), or ask to see scars or otherwise comment on the girls' appearance.) Self-injury is a behavior that results from a girl's (or boy's) inability to cope and adequately express her (or his) feelings. In this exercise, the girls will learn the difference between inside and outside feelings and how to express their deepest emotions in a positive manner.

MATERIALS

A T-shirt for every girl (this can be an old T-shirt, a gym shirt, etc.)
Safety pins
Index cards
Colored markers

PROCEDURE

1. Begin the group with a roundtable discussion about self-harm. Invite each member of the group to share her story.

   There will probably be some girls who have never self-injured. You should invite them to share a story about a friend or simply have them listen to others so they can learn about the behavior and how they can help someone who has self-injured.

2. When everyone has had a chance to speak, tell the girls that they are going to learn the difference between what they are feeling on the inside and how they show it on the outside.

3. Hand each girl a T-shirt and have her put it on inside out. Also hand out several index cards to each girl.

4. Ask the girls to think about what they (or others) might be feeling on the inside when they deliberately hurt themselves.

5. Have each girl write down one feeling per index card and safety-pin all the cards to her T-shirt.

6. When the girls have finished, have each one talk about the feelings on her T-shirt. Afterward, have each girl unpin her inside feelings off and turn her T-Shirt right side out.

7. Have each girl write down, on the back of each index card, how she can express on the outside what she is feeling on the inside in a healthy manner. For example, if the feeling is anger, she might write, "Go for a run" or "Hit a punching bag" on the card.

8. Encourage each girl to come up with multiple healthy alternatives to self-injury, then pin the cards to the outside of her shirt.

9. After they have all shared, instruct the girls to unpin their index cards. As they are doing this, begin a conversation about the importance of allowing others to see your true feelings and not hiding, or "stuffing," them. Point out that stuffing generally leads to an unhealthy decision.

10. Allow the girls to keep the index cards as a reminder of the healthy choices they came up with.

CLOSING QUESTIONS

❀ What did this activity mean to you? What have you learned about yourself?

❀ In the future, if you feel the need to self-injure and the healthy alternatives are just not working, whom can you call?

❀ How will you use what you have learned today in the future?

Tough Times

1. What do you think is the biggest issue facing teenage girls?

2. Have you or someone you know struggled with a mental health issue? Discuss.

3. What kind of experiences, if any, have had with death? How did you deal with them?

4. What do you do when you are really sad?

5. Talk about a time, or times, that you have felt alone and totally hopeless.

6. Do you think other people understand your situation?

7. A lot of girls cut themselves. Do you know anyone who has done this, or do you have any experiences with cutting?

8. Do you think that cutting, eating disorders, suicide attempts, and the like are done for attention?

9. People who cut sometimes say they do so to feel better. How do you think cutting relieves pain? What are some alternatives to cutting?

10. A big fear that people who cut have is that their parents or other adults will tell them they are "crazy" and should "just stop." What do you think about those remarks?

11. Talk about your home life: Do you have one parent or two? Assuming you had two parents when you were born, are they still together? Do you live in a happy household? Do you enjoy your family?

12. What do you think you would do if a friend of yours was suicidal?

13. Have you ever been put in a bad situation where you were really worried about a friend and felt that you needed to tell somebody, but swore you wouldn't?

14. When do you think it is OK to break a promise to a friend?

15. Do you think that people on medication are "crazy"?

16. How do you think that being a teenager today is tougher than it was for your parents?

17. What kinds of pressure are girls under that guys just don't understand?

18. Do you think physical pain is just as bad as mental pain?

19. When you are going through a tough time, whom can you reach out to?

20. What are some healthy things you can do to keep you sane when you are faced with a tough situation?

From *Girls in Real-Life Situations: Group Counseling Activities for Enhancing Social and Emotional Development—Grades 6–12*
© 2007 by J. V. Taylor and S. Trice-Black. Champaign, IL: Research Press. (800–519–2707, www.researchpress.com)

Think about It

Tough Times

Directions: Writing a letter is a powerful and cathartic way for you to connect with yourself and share your true feelings. For this exercise, take out a piece of paper and a pencil. Choose a letter to write from the following suggestions and let it all out! Don't give the letter to anybody. Either put it away in a safe place or rip it up and toss the pieces in the wastebasket when you are done.

1. Write a letter to yourself when you were younger, explaining that everything will be OK as you grow up.

2. Write a letter to the feeling or issue you have been struggling with, telling it to stop taking over your life. For example, you might decide to write a letter to your depression, your anger, your loneliness, your eating disorder, your chaotic mind, or your anxiety.

3. Write a letter to someone you have lost. Let this person know what is going on in your life and how much you miss him or her.

4. Write a letter to someone in your life you care about, and let the person know how you feel about him or her.

5. Write a letter to someone in your life you are having a problem with. Tell the person how you truly feel and how you need for him or her to change to help you.

6. Write a letter to a higher spiritual power that you believe in.

7. Write a letter to yourself in 10 years. Write what you think you will be doing and how much you have accomplished along the way.

Optional Journaling Questions

❀ Who do you wish could read your letter? Why?

❀ What makes your emotions toward somebody else feel so out of control?

From *Girls in Real-Life Situations: Group Counseling Activities for Enhancing Social and Emotional Development—Grades 6–12*
© 2007 by J. V. Taylor and S. Trice-Black. Champaign, IL: Research Press. (800–519–2707, www.researchpress.com)

Tough Times

Here are some great books for teens. Check them out!

* *Teenvirtue: Real Issues, Real Life: A Teen Girl's Survival Guide,* by Vicki Courtney (Nashville, TN: B&H Publishing Group, 2005).

* *The Truth about Forever,* by Sarah Dessen (Nashville, TN: Broadman and Holman Publishers, 2005).

* *Chicken Soup for the Preteen Soul: 101 Stories of Changes, Choices, and Growing Up,* by Jack Canfield, Mark Victor Hansen, Patty Hansen, Irene Dunlap, and Rusty Fischer (Deerfield Beach, FL: Health Communications, Inc., 2000).

* *When Nothing Matters Anymore: A Survival Guide for Depressed Teens,* by Bev Cobain (Minneapolis: Free Spirit Publishing, 2007).

* *Chicken Soup for the Teenage Soul on Tough Stuff: Stories of Tough Times and Lessons Learned,* by Jack Canfield, Mark Victor Hansen and Kimberly Kirberger (Deerfield Beach, FL: Health Communications, Inc., 2001).

From *Girls in Real-Life Situations: Group Counseling Activities for Enhancing Social and Emotional Development—Grades 6–12*
© 2007 by J. V. Taylor and S. Trice-Black. Champaign, IL: Research Press. (800–519–2707, www.researchpress.com)

Who I Am!

Connect!

Who I Am!

Time

10 minutes

Objective

For each girl to have the opportunity to share what she has learned about herself during the group sessions

Materials

None

Activity

Have each girl find a partner. Inform the girls that they will each have three minutes to talk and three minutes to listen. Have the partners choose which one will go first. The girl who is chosen must talk for three minutes, nonstop, about what she learned during G.I.R.L.S. and how she will pass that knowledge on to others. Her partner will engage in active listening and wait to speak until it is her turn. When three minutes are up, the listener will talk, and the talker will listen.

Process Question

❀ In a roundtable discussion, have each girl talk about what her partner learned.

My Mantra

RATIONALE

When negative thoughts cloud girls' brains, an uplifting thought, or mantra, can help boost their confidence. A mantra could be a song, a quote, an affirmation, a creed, a religious passage, or a simple positive reminder about the good things in life. In this activity, the girls will create their own personal mantras and design a collage to display them.

MATERIALS

A sheet of posterboard

Colored paper

Colored markers, colored pencils, glitter pens

Glue, scissors

Optional: A quote book, a Billboard Top 100 song list, magazines

PROCEDURE

1. Begin the activity by discussing the power of positive thought. Ask the girls to discuss their values or what they believe in.

2. Tell the girls that today they are going to create personal mantras.

3. Explain to them what a *mantra* is and give them a few moments to think about something they truly believe in. If possible, present them with different quotes, songs, or phrases that are uplifting.

4. Give the girls a sheet of colored paper and have them write down, creatively, what they want their mantra to be. Make sure they have enough time to make a wise decision and that their personal mantra is positive and easy to remember.

5. When they are done, allow each girl to share her new mantra with the group and explain why she chose it.

6. When all of the girls have had the opportunity to speak, have them create a collage of all of their mantras to display.

7. Discuss the importance of uplifting, positive self-talk, and make sure that each girl remembers her mantra.

CLOSING QUESTIONS

❀ What is powerful about your mantra?

❀ How will you use your mantra to help you in difficult times?

❀ How will you use what you have learned today in the future?

Compliment Journal

RATIONALE

Journaling is a great outlet for teens to use to understand themselves better. Teens often use journaling as a safe means of self-expression—nobody will judge their journaling, and the focus is on positive feelings and the upside of life. In this activity, the G.I.R.L.S. group will begin to create a compliment journal. In their journals, the girls will be instructed to keep track of the positive things that other people say about them. The goal is for them to home in on their strengths and listen more carefully for the good qualities that others see in them.

MATERIALS

A journal for each girl (notebook or loose-leaf binder)

Pencils or pens

Colored markers, glitter pens, colored pencils

PROCEDURE

1. Ask the girls to share some of the compliments they have received during the past week, as well as some of the compliments they have given during the past week.

2. Give each girl a journal and explain the concept: Encourage the girls to record, daily, the nice things that other people say to them and why they deserved that compliment. For example, if a girl is told that she played a really good soccer game last night, she might record the following in her journal:

   Compliment: I played a great game last night.

   Why I deserved it: I scored a goal and took the ball away three times.

3. Hand out the art materials and ask each girl to design a cover for her journal. While they work, have a discussion about the importance of focusing on the positive attributes that each girl has, as opposed to the criticisms that she may receive.

4. When the girls are done decorating their covers, instruct them to open their books to the first page and write their first name at the top.

5. Have each girl pass her journal around so the other group members can write a different compliment on that page (using no names).

6. Pass the journals around until each girl has written a compliment in every group member's journal.

CLOSING QUESTIONS

❀ What are the different areas in your life that result in your receiving compliments?

❀ If you are having a difficult time accepting a compliment, what are some things you can tell yourself to believe that you truly are deserving?

❀ How will you use what you have learned today in the future?

New Self-Portrait

RATIONALE

This lesson is similar to Self-Portrait, Session 3 in the "Who Am I?" sessions, and is repeated now to demonstrate progress. Self-portraits offer girls a creative and nonthreatening outlet to express how they view themselves. Because of their experience in G.I.R.L.S., it is hoped that they have a deeper understanding of themselves that can be expressed in a new self-portrait.

MATERIALS

A copy of the New Self-Portrait of _____ handout for each girl

Pencils or pens, colored markers

Scissors

Optional: glue, glitter

PROCEDURE

1. Spread out the art materials out so they are ready to use.
2. Tell the girls they will be drawing another self-portrait to see what, if anything, has changed in the way they perceive themselves.
3. Ask the girls to close their eyes and try to picture themselves.
4. Encourage the girls to think about how they feel about their body, home life, school, friends, and social activities.
5. Give the girls a few minutes to grasp an image.
6. Tell the girls that when they have an image, they should open their eyes and, to the best of their ability, put that image down on paper.
7. Allow the girls to talk freely with one another, but not about their self-portraits.
8. When they have all completed their drawings, ask each of them to describe her new self-portrait to the group.

CLOSING QUESTIONS

❀ Is your new self-portrait different from your first one? If so, what has changed? Is the change a positive or negative change?

❀ How will you let other people in your life know what is different about you? Do you anticipate any barriers or roadblocks?

❀ How will you use what you have learned today in the future?

New Self-Portrait of _____

From *Girls in Real-Life Situations: Group Counseling Activities for Enhancing Social and Emotional Development—Grades 6–12*
© 2007 by J. V. Taylor and S. Trice-Black. Champaign, IL: Research Press. (800–519–2707, www.researchpress.com)

In the Future, I...

RATIONALE

It is hoped that during the groups the girls have learned a great deal about themselves and what they want and need in their lives. Goal setting is a very helpful way for teens to break up huge, seemingly impossible projects into smaller, obtainable chunks. Setting and achieving small goals while striving to reach a large goal can be incredibly motivating because it heightens self-confidence as each smaller goal is achieved. In this activity, the girls will take what they have learned in the group and make an achievable goal out of it.

MATERIALS

A copy of the G.I.R.L.S. Goals handout for each girl

A copy of the Pretest/Posttest (p. 224), Group Evaluation (p. 226), and Certificate of Achievement (p. 233) for each girl

Pencils or pens

PROCEDURE

1. Begin by having a roundtable discussion about what the girls have learned in the group.

2. Have each girl share her favorite session and tell what she got out of it.

3. Explain to the girls that today they will be taking what they have learned and setting short-term goals to ensure that they are using their newfound life skills in every way possible! (You may have to explain the differences between short- and long-term goals.)

4. Give each girl a copy of the G.I.R.L.S. Goals handout and a pencil or pen.

5. Give the girls a few examples of good short-term goals while encouraging them to think about what they want or need. For example, "I will talk to my friends about my feelings instead of getting angry with them and ignoring them" or "I will eat healthier foods and exercise daily to take care of my body."

6. Allow the girls time to talk freely until everyone is finished.

7. Have each girl share and explain why she chose that particular goal.

8. Give each girl a copy of the Posttest and Group Evaluation. Have the girls quietly complete them.

9. Give each girl a G.I.R.L.S Certificate of Achievement and thank her for participating.

CLOSING QUESTIONS

❀ Why is goal setting important?

❀ How will you make sure that you reach your goal?

❀ How will you use what you have learned today in the future?

G.I.R.L.S. Goals

My goal _____

_____

Why did I choose this goal? _____

_____

When will I reach this goal? _____

_____

What is the first step? _____

_____

What is the second step? _____

_____

What is the third step? _____

_____

My reward for reaching my goal will be _____

_____

From *Girls in Real-Life Situations: Group Counseling Activities for Enhancing Social and Emotional Development—Grades 6–12*
© 2007 by J. V. Taylor and S. Trice-Black. Champaign, IL: Research Press. (800–519–2707, www.researchpress.com)

Who I Am!

1. Describe yourself.
2. What is your greatest strength?
3. What do you like best about your personality?
4. What have you learned about yourself in the G.I.R.L.S. group?
5. What choices do you make every day?
6. Talk about the people in your life whom you trust and can count on no matter what.
7. What are some ways that you can help others through tough times?
8. Talk about the best part about being a girl.
9. What are you looking forward to in the future?
10. Where do you see yourself in one year? Two? Five? Ten?
11. What expectations do you have of yourself? Are they realistic?
12. What keeps you and your friends bonded?
13. What characteristics do you look for in a friend? Have they changed since you started participating in the group?
14. When confronted with an uncomfortable situation, what can you do to assure that you come out feeling good about it?
15. What is femininity? Do you have to fulfill a particular role to feel feminine?
16. What is compromise? Do you have to win to feel good about a situation, or can you agree to disagree?
17. Do the media affect your identity? What are some ways that you can create your own identity?
18. Discuss some ways you can manage your stress and create a positive outlet to get some relief.
19. "When the going gets tough, the tough get going." Discuss this quote.
20. Talk about how you will make a difference in the world.

From *Girls in Real-Life Situations: Group Counseling Activities for Enhancing Social and Emotional Development—Grades 6–12*
© 2007 by J. V. Taylor and S. Trice-Black. Champaign, IL: Research Press. (800–519–2707, www.researchpress.com)

Think about It

Who I Am!

Directions: Write your name vertically in BIG letters on a separate sheet of paper, then come up with a positive adjective to describe yourself that begins with each letter of your name. Here are some adjectives that you might use:

open-minded	awesome	calm	cool
collected	fun	strong	adventurous
energetic	creative	smart	boisterous
playful	skilled	generous	magnificent
kind	nice	amazing	wonderful
compassionate	daring	helpful	imaginative
joyful	quaint	radical	tenacious

If you want, use your first, middle, and last names!

Here is an example:

Kind
Interesting
Energetic
Respectful
Sensitive
Tough
Entertaining
Noble

Tape the page with your name and the adjectives you chose to the inside of your locker or on your bedroom mirror—or keep it with you to remind yourself of how amazing you are!

Optional Journaling Questions
* What did you get the most out of in your G.I.R.L.S. experience?
* List what you have learned and how it will help you throughout your life?

From *Girls in Real-Life Situations: Group Counseling Activities for Enhancing Social and Emotional Development—Grades 6–12*
© 2007 by J. V. Taylor and S. Trice-Black. Champaign, IL: Research Press. (800–519–2707, www.researchpress.com)

Check It Out

Who I Am!

Here are some great books for teens. Check them out!

❀ *33 Things Every Girl Should Know: Stories, Songs, Poems, and Smart Talk by 33 Extraordinary Women,* by Tonya Bolden (New York: Crown Publishers, 1998).

❀ *Don't Sweat the Small Stuff for Teens,* by Richard Carlson (New York: Hyperion, 2000).

❀ *Teens Can Make It Happen: Nine Steps for Success,* by Stedman Graham (New York: Fireside, 2000).

❀ *Teens Can Make It Happen Workbook,* by Stedman Graham (New York: Fireside, 2001).

❀ *The Girls' Book of Wisdom: Empowering, Inspirational Quotes from Over 400 Fabulous Females,* by Catherine Dee and Ali Douglas (Lebanon, IN: Little, Brown Young Readers, 1999).

From *Girls in Real-Life Situations: Group Counseling Activities for Enhancing Social and Emotional Development—Grades 6–12*
© 2007 by J. V. Taylor and S. Trice-Black. Champaign, IL: Research Press. (800–519–2707, www.researchpress.com)

Appendixes

G.I.R.L.S. Parent/Guardian Consent Form

To the parent/guardian of _____:

The intention of this letter is to invite your daughter to participate in the small-group experience Girls in Real-Life Situations (G.I.R.L.S.). The purpose of G.I.R.L.S. is to help your daughter discuss and deal with issues and situations that girls often face during their teenage years. In addition, G.I.R.L.S. will provide your daughter with the opportunity to openly discuss these issues in a safe and supportive environment.

G.I.R.L.S. will meet at _____ on the following dates and times:

_____

_____

Please complete the consent form below, placing a check mark in the appropriate box, and return it to me by _____. If you have any questions, please do not hesitate to call me at _____.

Sincerely,

G.I.R.L.S. facilitator

☐ I **grant** permission for my daughter to participate in G.I.R.L.S.

☐ I **deny** permission for my daughter to participate in G.I.R.L.S.

Daughter's name _____ Parent/guardian name _____

Parent/guardian signature _____ Date _____

Home phone number _____ Work phone number _____

From *Girls in Real-Life Situations: Group Counseling Activities for Enhancing Social and Emotional Development—Grades 6–12*
© 2007 by J. V. Taylor and S. Trice-Black. Champaign, IL: Research Press. (800–519–2707, www.researchpress.com)

G.I.R.L.S. Confidentiality Pledge

Dear G.I.R.L.S. Member:

Congratulations on your willingness to participate in G.I.R.L.S. During the group sessions, we will be discussing many issues that are important and sacred to all adolescent and teenage girls. In the group environment, you will be asked to share stories and information and provide help and feedback to other group members. The most important rule in G.I.R.L.S. is confidentiality. *Confidentiality* means that you do not discuss what another member has said to anyone whenever you are outside of the group setting or not in the presence of the group facilitator. As long as nobody else can overhear, you may talk about the group with your parent or guardian or other group members. *If you break confidentiality, you may be asked to leave the group.* Please think carefully about this issue and sign the pledge below if you agree to follow the requirements of the confidentiality agreement.

I, _____, understand what confidentiality means, and I promise that I will not reveal any information about another group member to anyone outside of the group, except my parent or guardian. If I choose to break this confidentiality agreement, I understand that I may be asked to leave the group.

Your signature _____ Date _____

From *Girls in Real-Life Situations: Group Counseling Activities for Enhancing Social and Emotional Development—Grades 6–12*
© 2007 by J. V. Taylor and S. Trice-Black. Champaign, IL: Research Press. (800–519–2707, www.researchpress.com)

G.I.R.L.S. Certificate of Achievement

CONGRATULATIONS

Name _____

You have been an awesome contributor to the success of Girls in Real-Life Situations.

You now have the tools, skills, and confidence to make a difference to girls everywhere.

Spread your sunshine and bloom where you are planted!

G.I.R.L.S. facilitator _____ Date _____

From *Girls in Real-Life Situations: Group Counseling Activities for Enhancing Social and Emotional Development—Grades 6–12*
© 2007 by J. V. Taylor and S. Trice-Black. Champaign, IL: Research Press. (800–519–2707, www.researchpress.com)

G.I.R.L.S. Pretest/Posttest

Name _____ Date _____

Directions: Read the following questions and choose only one answer. Think about your answers and be really honest with yourself!

1. I feel that I know myself and the things that make me happy.
   a. Yes
   b. No
   c. Sometimes

2. I am happy with the way my body looks.
   a. Yes
   b. No
   c. Sometimes

3. I practice good decision-making skills and don't feel pressure from my friends to do things I don't want to.
   a. Yes
   b. No
   c. Sometimes

4. I feel that I can talk openly to my friends and family about my true feelings.
   a. Yes
   b. No
   c. Sometimes

5. I am in touch with my emotions and always know how I am really feeling.
   a. Yes
   b. No
   c. Sometimes

6. I feel that I am always a good friend and can be trusted.
   a. Yes
   b. No
   c. Sometimes

From *Girls in Real-Life Situations: Group Counseling Activities for Enhancing Social and Emotional Development—Grades 6–12*
© 2007 by J. V. Taylor and S. Trice-Black. Champaign, IL: Research Press. (800–519–2707, www.researchpress.com)

Appendix D

7. I know who I want to date or "go out with" and choose them according to what I like.
    a. Yes
    b. No
    c. Sometimes

8. I feel good about myself.
    a. Yes
    b. No
    c. Sometimes

9. I know how to handle stress.
    a. Yes
    b. No
    c. Sometimes

10. I know who to go to when I need support.
    a. Yes
    b. No
    c. Sometimes

11. I know that other girls often have trouble with the same issues that I do.
    a. Yes
    b. No
    c. Sometimes

12. I am confident, secure, and know that I am an important part of this world.
    a. Yes
    b. No
    c. Sometimes

G.I.R.L.S. Group Evaluation

1. Did you learn anything from G.I.R.L.S.?
   ❏ Yes   ❏ No
   If yes, what did you learn?

   _____

   _____

   _____

2. What was the most helpful part of G.I.R.L.S.?

   _____

   _____

   _____

3. What was the least helpful part of G.I.R.L.S.?

   _____

   _____

   _____

4. Did you feel heard by the other girls in the group?
   ❏ Yes   ❏ No
   Why or why not?

   _____

   _____

   _____

From *Girls in Real-Life Situations: Group Counseling Activities for Enhancing Social and Emotional Development—Grades 6–12*
© 2007 by J. V. Taylor and S. Trice-Black. Champaign, IL: Research Press. (800–519–2707, www.researchpress.com)

G.I.R.L.S. Group Evaluation (continued)

5. Did you feel comfortable sharing personal information about yourself with the group?
   ❑ Yes   ❑ No
   Why or why not?

   _____

   _____

   _____

6. Did you complete the "Think about It" worksheets on your own time?
   ❑ Yes   ❑ No
   If yes, did you find them helpful?
   ❑ Yes   ❑ Kind of   ❑ No

7. Did you keep a journal?
   ❑ Yes   ❑ Kind of   ❑ No
   If yes, will you continue to journal?
   ❑ Yes   ❑ No

8. Would you recommend this group to a friend?
   ❑ Yes   ❑ No

About the Authors

JULIA V. TAYLOR is a professional school counselor for Wake County Public Schools in Raleigh, North Carolina. Originating from the Washington, D.C., area, she received her undergraduate degree from George Mason University in Fairfax, Virginia, and her master's degree from Marymount University in Arlington, Virginia. She has been a counselor at both the middle school and high school levels. Julia has presented her research on relational aggression at numerous local and national conferences, inservices, and workshops. She has conducted television, newspaper, and documentary interviews, along with authoring numerous publications about adolescent and parenting issues. Julia is the professional interest network bullying specialist for the American School Counselor Association and serves on the North Carolina School Counselor Association Board. In addition to speaking to professionals, Julia frequently educates children, teens, and parents in local communities about relational aggression, body image, and other adolescent/teen issues.

SHANNON TRICE-BLACK received her bachelor's degree from the College of William and Mary and her master's degree in counselor education from the University of Virginia. She worked as a school counselor for 10 years at the elementary and middle school levels before returning to the University of Virginia, where she is currently a doctoral student in counseling education. Shannon continues to maintain a small part-time counseling practice, working with children, adolescents, and adults. It is her passion for school counseling that inspires her to assist others in reaching the needs of every student. Shannon has presented her work and writings on classroom guidance, bullying, and relational aggression at conferences, workshops, and master's level classes. She serves on the board of the Jefferson Counseling Association and the Virginia Association for Counselor Education and Supervision. In addition, Shannon is a member of the Virginia Counselors Association, Virginia School Counselors Association, American Counseling Association, and Chi Sigma Iota. She lives in Goochland, Virginia, with her husband and two daughters.